STORY OF OUR LEGENDS

MADE IN PARADISE
CONTENTS

- 04 Introduction by Brendan Rodgers
- 06 Jock Stein Stand Banner
- 08 **Jimmy Johnstone**
- 10 Dixie Deans
- 11 **Johnny Doyle**
- 12 Kenny Dalglish
- 13 **John Collins**
- 14 John Hughes
- 15 **Famous Five - Celtic's first game**
- 16 Stevie Chalmers
- 18 **Bobby Murdoch**
- 20 Neilly Mochan
- 21 **John Fallon**
- 22 Jimmy McGrory
- 24 **Jim Craig**
- 26 Bobby Lennox
- 28 **Pat Bonner**
- 29 Roy Aitken
- 30 **Chris Sutton**
- 31 Sandy McMahon
- 32 **Stiliyan Petrov**
- 34 Jimmy Delaney
- 35 **Brian McClair**
- 36 Charlie Tully
- 37 **Jackie McNamara**
- 38 Patsy Gallacher
- 40 **Davie Hay**
- 41 Paul Lambert
- 42 **Alec McNair**
- 43 Famous Five - Hampden in the Sun
- 44 **Paul McStay**
- 46 Neil Lennon
- 48 **Willie Fernie**
- 49 Famous Five - Champions of Europe
- 50 **Lisbon Lions Stand Banner**
- 52 Ronnie Simpson
- 54 **Danny McGrain**
- 56 Willie Wallace
- 58 **Peter Grant**
- 59 Willie O'Neill
- 60 **Murdo MacLeod**
- 61 Lubo Moravcik
- 62 **John Clark**
- 64 Bertie Peacock
- 65 **Tom Boyd**
- 66 Bobby Evans
- 67 **Jimmy McMenemy**
- 68 John Hartson
- 69 **Famous Five - Stopping the 10**
- 70 Billy McNeill
- 72 **Jock Stein**
- 73 John Thomson
- 74 **Tommy Gemmell**
- 76 Willie Maley
- 78 **Jimmy Quinn**
- 79 Charlie Gallagher
- 80 **Henrik Larsson**
- 82 Famous Five - Beating Barcelona
- 83 **Johnny Crum**
- 84 Scott Brown
- 86 **Tommy Burns**
- 88 Jim Brogan
- 89 **Joe McBride**
- 90 Bertie Auld
- 92 **Sean Fallon**
- 93 Shunsuke Nakamura
- 95 **Statistics**

Celtic Football Club
Celtic Park, Glasgow G40 3RE

Celtic plc Directors
Ian Bankier, Peter Lawwell,
Eric Riley, Dermot Desmond, Tom Allison,
Brian Wilson, Ian Livingston, Chris McKay
CFAC Directors Peter Lawwell, Eric Riley,
John Keane, Michael McDonald,
Kevin Sweeney
Honorary Chairman CFAC John Keane

Manager Brendan Rodgers
Assistant Manager Chris Davies
Head of Performance Glen Driscoll
First-team coach John Kennedy
Football Development Manager John Park
Head of Youth Chris McCart
Head Physiotherapist Tim Williamson
Kit Controller John Clark

Contact
Celtic Football Club 0871 226 1888
(Calls cost 13p per minute, plus your phone company's access charge. For customer enquiries relating to existing purchases only, please call 0141 230 1967. Calls charged at standard rate.)

Celtic Football Club Editorial
Editorial 0141 551 4264
Editor Paul Cuddihy
Deputy Editor Joe Sullivan
Writers Mark Henderson, Martin Dalziel

Published by Sport Media
Managing Director Steve Hanrahan
Executive Art Editor Rick Cooke
Senior Editor Paul Dove
Production Editor Michael McGuinness
Design Lee Ashun, Alison Barkley,
Colin Sumpter, Colin Harrison,
Graeme Helliwell, Lisa Critchley, Glen Hind
Marketing and Communications Manager
Claire Brown
Photography PA Photos, SNS Pix
Printed by Buxton Press

All content in the Celtic View is copyright of Celtic FC Limited and must not be reprinted without prior written consent of Celtic FC Limited

© Trinity Mirror Sport Media. All rights reserved. No part of this publication may be reproduced by any means without the written permission of the Copyright owners. Although every effort has been made to ensure the accuracy of this publication, the publishers cannot accept responsibility for errors or omissions. In the interest of independence and impartiality, many features in this publication have been written by third-party experts. It should be noted that any opinions expressed therein are the views of the writers themselves and not necessarily those of Celtic FC. Terms and conditions for all competitions appearing in this magazine are available on request. ISBN: 9781910335437

STORY OF OUR LEGENDS

THIS IS PARADISE

Celtic Park is a special place, famous throughout the world for the incredible atmosphere that our fans generate in support of the team. Many of the world's best players have said over the years that there's nowhere like it to play football, and that feeling is something I hope we can generate in the seasons ahead, both in our domestic fixtures but also on the European stage.

Paradise is also a place where, like the banners at either end of the stadium proclaim, legends are made. We know their names and the incredible things they've done for our club. Some of them we've read about or heard from older relatives and friends who've brought us up to support this wonderful club, while others we've been lucky enough to witness at close hand. But we should be thankful that every single one of them wore our jersey with pride and distinction, and played football the Celtic way.

Making your way to Celtic Park is always an exciting journey for every supporter, full of anticipation for the 90 minutes ahead, and all of us can remember these occasions – the great games we've seen and the wonderful players we've cheered. The front of the stadium is stunning, with the Celtic Way welcoming visitors to Paradise, while the banners adorning the main stand pay tribute to just a few of the many highlights from our history.

The banners outside both the Jock Stein Stand and the Lisbon Lions Stand are also there in tribute to some of our greatest ever players, from famous names like Jimmy Quinn, Patsy Gallacher and Jimmy McGrory, through to Charlie Tully, Bertie Peacock, the legendary Lisbon Lions, and then to great Celts like Danny McGrain, Kenny Dalglish, Tommy Burns and Paul McStay. And not forgetting, of course, more recent Celts like Henrik Larsson, Lubo Moravick, Shunsuke Nakamura and our club captain, Scott Brown.

They are there to remind us of our history – and we have so many great moments to remember – and also act as an inspiration for the current players

We can be inspired by the men who've gone before us to write our own chapter in the Celtic history books

and ones in the future who will be lucky enough to wear the green and white Hoops.

That's what this Paradise Legends magazine is doing too – celebrating our wonderful history and the men who've ensured that Celtic Football Club is a name that is known throughout the world.

The aim of everyone here at the football club is to bring success to our supporters, and we will be doing everything we can to achieve that. We can be inspired by the men who've gone before us, and what they did for the club, and their contribution only makes us even more determined to write our own chapter in the Celtic history books that will hopefully be remembered and celebrated for many generations to come.

Brendan Rodgers
Manager
Celtic Football Club

CELTIC FOOTBALL CLUB 1888
new balance
CELTIC

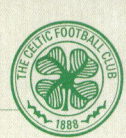

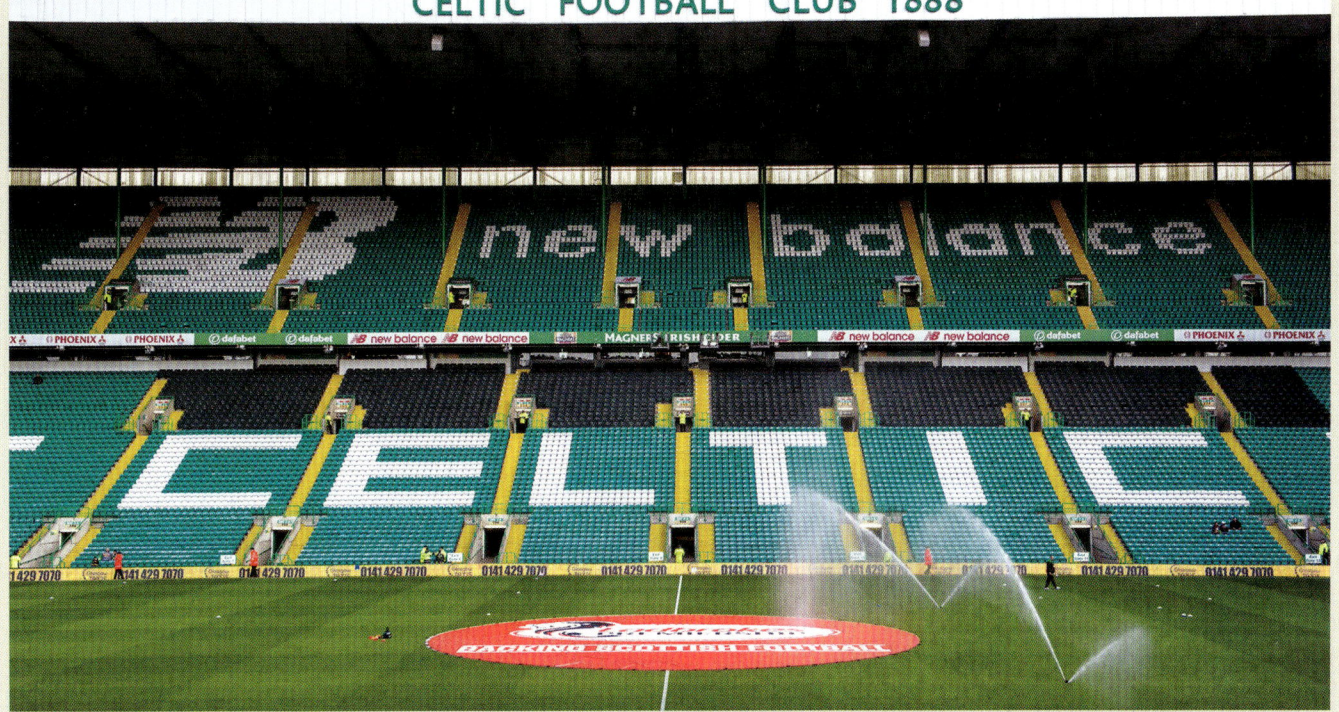

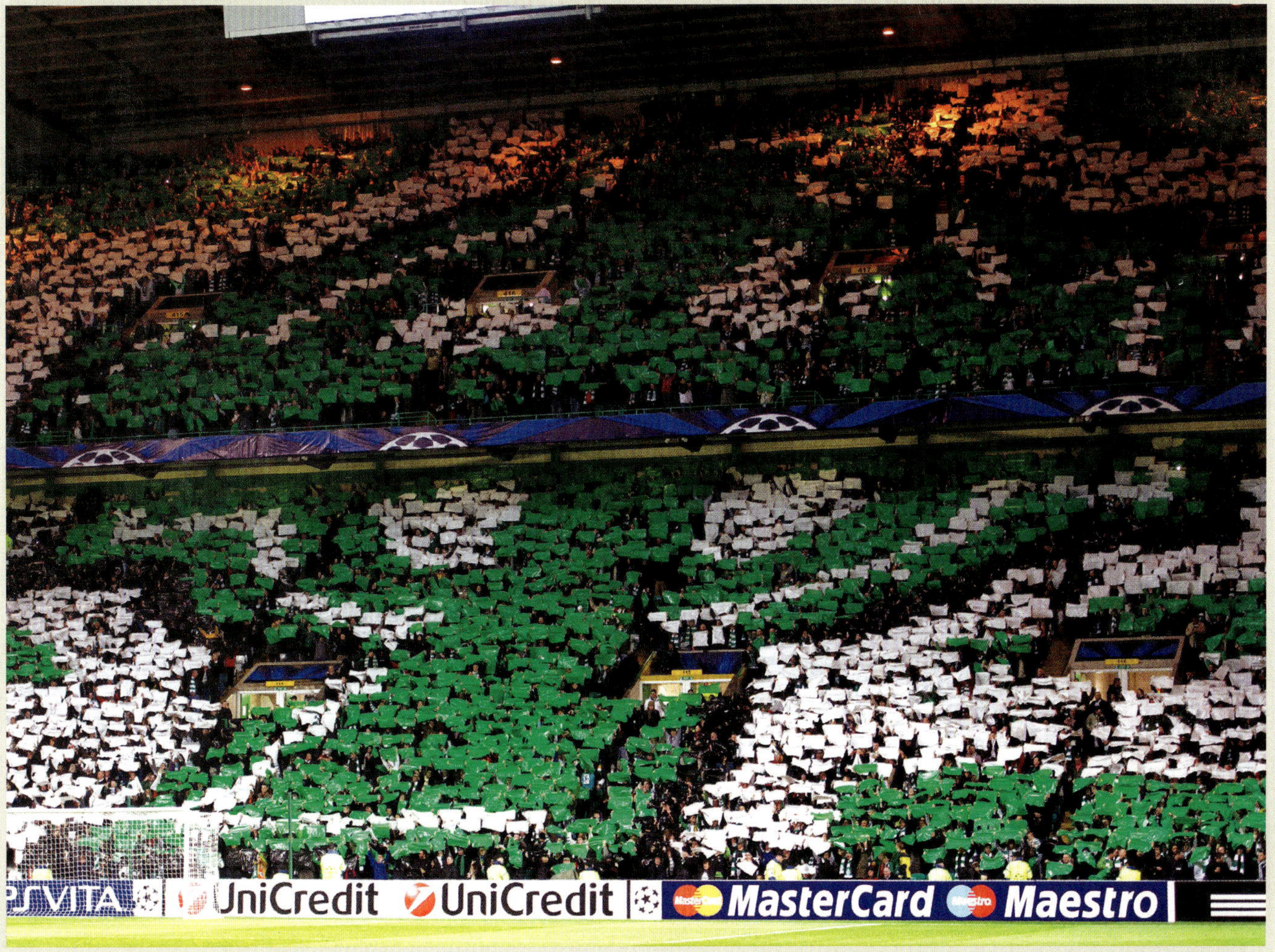
UniCredit
UniCredit
MasterCard
Maestro

STORY OF OUR LEGENDS

JOCK STEIN

Stand

STORY OF OUR LEGENDS

JIMMY JOHNSTONE

1961 - 1975

JIMMY JOHNSTONE

WINGER
Celtic debut: March 27, 1963, League, Kilmarnock 6-0 Celtic

	App	Subs	Goals
League	298	10	82
Scottish Cup	47	1	11
League Cup	87	5	21
Europe	66	1	16
Total	**498**	**17**	**130**

He was, is and always will be the Greatest Ever Celt. Jimmy Johnstone, known and loved by the Celtic Family as 'Jinky', received that accolade back in 2002. It was one that was thoroughly deserved. He was the very definition of a mercurial talent, and while his ability with a ball marked him out as a unique player, his skills were harnessed for the good of the team. A Viewpark Bhoy, Jinky joined Blantyre Celtic in 1960 but his shock of red hair had already been noted by patrons of The Jungle when he was a ballboy at Celtic Park. Celtic would always have been favourites to capture his signature but news that Manchester United were sniffing around hurried up that process and he signed on November 8, 1961, just a few weeks after his 17th birthday.

On the evening of Wednesday, March 27, 1963, an injury-ravaged Celtic side travelled to Rugby Park to take on a high-flying Kilmarnock side they had already drawn 1-1 with back in October. The already young and inexperienced Celtic team fielded featured three debutants in the shape of third-choice keeper, Dick Madden, centre-back John Cushley and the diminutive Jimmy Johnstone on the right-wing, and it was a tough debut for the young Celts as Kilmarnock won 6-0.

08 | Made In Paradise

JIMMY JOHNSTONE

His career was littered with highs and there was a plethora of games where he just literally tore teams apart – sometimes seemingly single-handed

However, for Jimmy Johnstone, it wasn't a prelude to the rest of his Celtic career. He won nine championship medals, four in the Scottish Cup, five in the League Cup and, the pinnacle of them all, the European Cup in 1967.

His career, though, was littered with highs and there was a plethora of games where he just literally tore teams apart – sometimes seemingly single-handed. There was Alfredo Di Stefano's testimonial in 1967 when 120,000 Real Madrid fans chanted 'Ole' every time Jinky bamboozled one of their own players. There was the famed Red Star Belgrade game when, with the game tied 1-1 at half-time, Jock Stein told Johnstone, who had a chronic fear of flying, that if the Hoops won by four clear goals then he wouldn't have to travel to Belgrade – Jinky ran amok and scored twice, the second of those coming nine minutes from the end in Celtic's 5-1 master-class.

Then there was the 1970 European Cup semi-final when he corkscrewed the best Leeds United had to offer into the Hampden turf.

The courage and bravery that Jimmy Johnstone displayed throughout his playing career, often in the face of extreme physical intimidation from his opponents, also came to the fore when he was diagnosed with Motor Neurone Disease, and his brave fight against that terrible illness was an example and inspiration to all.

Sadly, he lost that battle in March 2006, but he remains an integral part of Celtic Football Club, immortalised in the statue standing at the front of Celtic Park, and remembered in the memories of everyone who was lucky enough to see him play, and for those younger supporters who have been imbued with tales of the wee red-haired winger who had the heart of a Lion and football skills that were a gift from God.

STORY OF OUR LEGENDS

DIXIE DEANS
1971 - 1976

When Celtic signed Dixie Deans from Motherwell in October 1971, the striker was still to serve four weeks of a six-week ban when he completed his transfer. Not only could he not play for four weeks but it also cost the Hoops a fine. Despite having a reputation for being one of the bad boys of Scottish football while at Motherwell, Deans knuckled down and was only given his marching orders once while wearing the green and white Hoops, and this came in a reserve match.

And having served his suspension, Deans made his debut in a league game against Partick Thistle at Firhill and he capped it by scoring Celtic's fifth and final goal of the afternoon with just four minutes of the match remaining.

Deans' debut season of 1971/72 proved to be an eventful one for the player, and the club too. He joined just after the disastrous League Cup final when the Hoops lost 4-1 to Partick Thistle at Hampden, but would help his new team secure a league and cup double, which saw him hit a hat-trick against Hibernian in a 6-1 Scottish Cup final triumph.

He also endured penalty shoot-out agony in the European Cup semi-final against Inter Milan, as he blazed his spot-kick over the bar, allowing the Italians to progress to the final. Three days later, he ran out at Celtic Park to face his old club, Motherwell, and he was given a standing ovation by the Celtic support. Deans repaid them with two of Celtic's five goals in a 5-2 success, though he declined to take either of the two penalties the Hoops were awarded – Bobby Murdoch converted both of them.

Deans was a prolific goalscorer, scoring 124 goals in 184 matches, which included seven hat-tricks. As well as his 1972 Scottish Cup final treble against Hibs, he also netted a hat-trick against the Edinburgh side two years later in the League Cup final.

Among his other goalscoring feats, he once scored six goals in a single game. That came against Partick Thistle in 1973, and it's the closest any Celtic player has come to equaling Jimmy McGrory's eight goals that he scored in a game against Dunfermline Athletic back in 1928. McGrory was actually at the game and congratulated Deans afterwards.

His last goal for the Hoops came, ironically, from the penalty spot in a game against Ayr United in April 1976, and he would play one more game for the club before he left for Luton Town.

He also has the distinction of being the last Celtic player to score a goal for the Hoops on Christmas Day. That came against Hearts on December 25, 1971 and it proved to be the winner as Jock Stein's side ran out 3-2 winners. An impressive crowd of 34,000 made it along to Celtic Park for the festive football.

DIXIE DEANS

FORWARD
Celtic debut:
November 27, 1971, League,
Partick Thistle 1-5 Celtic
(scored once)

	App	Subs	Goals
League	122	5	89
Scottish Cup	21	0	18
League Cup	21	1	11
Europe	11	3	6
Total	**175**	**9**	**124**

JOHNNY DOYLE

1976 - 1981

It was on March 15, 1976 that Johnny Doyle fulfilled a dream when he signed for his beloved Celtic Football Club. He was a Celtic supporter. He remained so throughout his all-too-short life, never forgetting this fact or that he felt proud and privileged to wear the green and white Hoops.

He was a player of undoubted quality, while his evident passion for the cause was there for all to see – sometimes he would see red because of it – and he was always a favourite with the Celtic fans for those reasons and, more importantly, because they recognised in him one of their own.

If he hadn't been playing for the team, he would have been standing alongside them on the terraces. Indeed, Doyle would go to games, as a Celtic player, wearing a Celtic scarf, so that if he wasn't selected, he could join his fellow fans in cheering on the team.

Johnny Doyle was a Viewpark Bhoy, born on May 11, 1951, and like another famous Viewpark winger, Jimmy Johnstone, Doyle would also wear the green and white Hoops.

His route to Paradise was not a straight one, however. He joined Ayr United in 1968 and spent eight years at Somerset Park before he got his move to Celtic Park.

He joined his boyhood heroes on March 15, 1976, and made his debut just five days later at Dens Park in a 1-0 victory for Jock Stein's side, the only goal of the game coming from Kenny Dalglish.

It would be the following season that he began to establish himself in the first-team, and he netted the first of 37 goals in a 3-0 League Cup sectional win over Dumbarton.

He was a regular in the side as Stein steered the club to an impressive league and Scottish Cup double, with Doyle and Tommy Burns the substitutes in the cup final victory over Rangers.

Between 1976 and 1981, Johnny Doyle made 123 appearances for Celtic, scoring 37 goals including, perhaps most memorably a header in the 2-0 victory over Real Madrid in the European Cup quarter-final in 1980.

In the famous '10 men won the league' game in May 1979, Doyle was the 11th man, red-carded early in the second-half against Rangers. He was the most relieved man at Celtic Park when his team-mates won the game 4-2 to clinch the title.

Johnny Doyle was only 30-years-old when he died, on October 19, 1981, the result of a tragic accident while he was working in his house.

He was mourned as a husband, father, brother, friend and team-mate by all who knew him, while the Celtic support mourned his loss as a fellow Celt.

And the words of Tommy Burns, speaking to the *Celtic View* in 2005 about his friend, have a particular poignancy. "It was a tragedy when Doyley died, and it makes you realise just how fortunate you are when there are people who come into this world and then leave it so suddenly."

JOHNNY DOYLE

FORWARD
Celtic debut:
March 20, 1976,
League,
Dundee 0-1 Celtic

	App	Subs	Goals
League	82	13	15
Scottish Cup	10	2	7
League Cup	25	4	14
Europe	6	1	1
Total	**123**	**20**	**37**

MADE IN PARADISE | 11

STORY OF OUR LEGENDS

KENNY DALGLISH

1967 - 1977

Kenny Dalglish might have famously torn down posters of Rangers players on his bedroom wall when then Celtic assistant manager, Sean Fallon, turned up at the family home near Ibrox to sign the talented teenager in 1967, but having committed his football future to the green and white Hoops, Dalglish would go on to establish himself as a Celtic great over the next decade. That his departure to Liverpool in 1977 devastated the Celtic support is a sign of his popularity and importance to the team.

Dalglish was part of an exceptionally talented reserve team known as the Quality Street Gang, alongside the likes of Danny McGrain, Davie Hay, George Connelly and Lou Macari.

Having spent some time out on loan at Cumbernauld United, Dalglish returned to Celtic Park and made his debut in the second leg of the League Cup quarter final against Hamilton Accies in September 1968. The Hoops were already leading 10-0 from the first leg, and 17-year-old Dalglish came on as a substitute for Charlie Gallagher, who was making his last appearance for the club.

There were many highs during Kenny Dalglish's 10-year career with Celtic, including winning four league championships, four Scottish Cups and the League Cup as well as captaining the Hoops, but his real breakthrough to the first team in the opening months of the 1971/72 season was astronomical. Because of reconstruction work at Celtic Park, the Hoops' 'home' League Cup opener against Rangers went ahead at Ibrox – the first of three Celtic games there in little more than three weeks. Celtic won the League Cup encounters 2-0 and 3-0 as well as winning the league clash by 3-2 – and 20-year-old Kenny Dalglish scored in all three games! And the highs just kept on coming.

In his last season at the club, he helped Celtic to a league and Scottish Cup double as well as losing out by a solitary goal after extra-time in the League Cup final to Aberdeen – a game in which he scored for the Hoops. He captained the Hoops to the title with five games to go and raised the Scottish Cup aloft on May 7 with one league game left to play on the Tuesday night at Fir Park.

On May 10, 1977, Motherwell took a 2-0 half-time lead but 20-year-old Tommy Burns pulled one back on the hour mark and in the 69th minute it was Dalglish who equalised with his 167th and last goal in his 320th and last competitive game for the Hoops.

On August 9, 1977, in a friendly at Dunfermline, Celtic wore a badge on the Hoops for the first time ever and Jock Stein also watched Kenny Dalglish wear a Celtic badge for the first and last time. The next day he had moved to Liverpool in a British record £440,000 deal. To add to his medal haul with Celtic, in the red of Liverpool he lifted six championships, two FA Cups, four League Cups, seven Charity Shields and three European Cups as well as one UEFA Super Cup. In management with Liverpool he won three championships, two FA Cups, one League Cup (in his second spell) and four Charity Shields. As boss at Blackburn Rovers he won the championship before taking up the post of manager at Newcastle United. He also returned to Celtic with John Barnes and was in charge of the team when the Hoops lifted the League Cup in 2000.

KENNY DALGLISH

FORWARD
Celtic debut:
September 25, 1968,
League Cup,
Hamilton Accies 2-4 Celtic

	App	Subs	Goals
League	200	4	112
Scottish Cup	30	0	11
League Cup	56	3	35
Europe	27	0	9
Total	**313**	**7**	**167**

JOHN COLLINS
1990 - 1996

JOHN COLLINS

MIDFIELDER
Celtic debut:
August 22, 1990
League Cup
Celtic 4-0 Airdrie

	App	Subs	Goals
League	211	6	47
Scottish Cup	21	0	3
League Cup	22	0	3
Europe	13	0	1
Total	**267**	**6**	**54**

Galashiels-born John Collins played for Celtic Boys' Club as a youngster and his father drove him up from the Borders every week for training and games but as a matter of necessity he switched to East Coast club, Hutchison Vale.

He joined Hibernian on turning 16-years-old in January 1984 making his first-team debut in the 1985/86 season and came on as a substitute in that term's unsuccessful League Cup final against Aberdeen at Hampden.

The youngster became noted as a cultured midfielder in his six years at Easter Road and his tussles with Paul McStay when Hibs played Celtic produced some of the most intriguing encounters in Scottish football as two of the country's most talented footballers came head-to-head.

As absorbing as those combats were, by the summer of 1990, they would be no more as Celtic paid a then club record fee for the player and John Collins became the first million-pound player to move between Scottish clubs.

The two midfield masters of Scottish football no longer faced each other in a battle of the greens but teamed up as central figures in the Celtic team of the early 1990s to such effect that we can only wonder what the unproductive side of those years would have been like without them both together in the same team.

It was a barren era as far as trophies went for Celtic but, when Tommy Burns arrived as manager in 1994, much of the silky soccer displayed by the side revolved around McStay and Collins.

The only success of those times was the Scottish Cup victory over Airdrie at Hampden in 1995 and it's a travesty that this was McStay's only silverware as captain and the only trophy won by Collins as a Celt, such was their standing in the game.

A feature of Collins' game were his trademark long-range free-kicks with two against Rangers in different away games real standouts because of the swerve he put on the ball – one of the goals coming in the infamous lock-out game of April, 1994 when he silenced an Ibrox devoid of Celtic fans because of a ban imposed by the home club.

Still, it didn't stop a hired plane from flying overhead trailing a banner proclaiming, "Hail, Hail the Celts are here!"

He also represented Scotland 58 times including appearing in Euro '96 and the World Cup of 1998 when he scored from the penalty spot against Brazil – one of the 12 goals he scored for the national side.

Collins moved on to Monaco in 1996 and returned across the channel to play for Everton and then Fulham where he also took up coaching duties with the London club.

In management, he won the League Cup with Hibernian in 2007 before moving to Charleroi in Belgium the following year. Back in Scotland, Collins was appointed Director of Football at Livingston and went on to further coaching work with the SFA before returning to Celtic once more.

When Ronny Deila arrived as Celtic manager in 2014, John Collins was named as assistant manager and departed with the Norwegian after winning two successive league championships and a League Cup.

MADE IN PARADISE | 13

STORY OF OUR LEGENDS

JOHN HUGHES

1959 - 1971

John Hughes is Celtic's seventh top scorer of all-time, with 188 goals for the Hoops in 383 appearances. He scored on his debut in a League Cup tie against Third Lanark, and he would net a total of 14 goals that season in all competitions. Only Stevie Chalmers scored more goals that term, though the following season, only Hughes' second as a Celt, he scored 26 goals to be the club's top scorer.

Having come through the ranks at the club, he was one of a clutch of promising young players on which the hopes of the club rested, and having suffered through his early years at the club from a lack of success, Hughes was in the Celtic team which lifted the Scottish Cup in 1965 with a 3-2 victory over Dunfermline Athletic, a triumph which ushered in a golden era under Jock Stein.

Hughes never had the easiest of relationships with the Celtic manager, and having played in five of the eight games which took the club to the European Cup final in 1967, he might have expected a starting berth in Lisbon.

That didn't happen, much to the player's disappointment. He was in the starting XI for the 1970 European Cup final, but that game would end in defeat for the Hoops.

A Coatbridge Bhoy, born on April 3, 1943, Hughes starred for St Augustine's School before blazing a trail with Kirkshaw Amateurs and Junior side, Shotts Bon Accord. It was from there that he made the move to the team he had always supported and he joined Celtic on October 3, 1959 at the age of just 16. It wouldn't take this towering striker long to make the step up to the first team.

A week after making his goalscoring debut against Third Lanark, Hughes ran Rangers ragged in the same competition at Ibrox and scored what proved to be the winner in a 3-2 victory for the Hoops watched by a crowd of 60,000.

He had six championship wins, all of them in a row and he also played in the game that kick-started the glory years under Jock Stein, the 3-2 Scottish Cup final win over Dunfermline in 1965. He also played in four League Cup-winning teams, the first three successively and the first of those featured two Hughes penalties in a 2-1 victory over Rangers watched by 107,600. As far as individual performances go, though, there was his glancing header to put Celtic back in the driving seat on aggregate against Leeds United in the 1970 European Cup semi-final at Hampden as 136,505 looked on.

However, in domestic terms, the red letter day was a performance against Aberdeen on January 30, 1965 when he borrowed Billy McNeill's

He borrowed Billy McNeill's sandshoes to play on the icy rock hard surface and scored FIVE goals in the 8-0 win!

sandshoes to play on the icy rock-hard surface and scored **FIVE** goals in the 8-0 win!

He moved to Crystal Palace in October 1971 at the age of 27, a move that both surprised and disappointed him.

John Hughes was known as 'Yogi' and although the genesis of this is debated – a likeness to Yogi Bear, or, in the slogan of the cartoon character, he was 'smarter than the average bear', or he got lost in the woods on one of Neilly Mochan's legendary pre-European match walks before emerging from the undergrowth unharmed – it did lead to the 'Feed the Bear' chant that also later served Roy Aitken.

JOHN HUGHES

FORWARD
Celtic debut: August 13, 1960, League Cup, Celtic 2-0 Third Lanark (scored once)

	App	Subs	Goals
League	233	3	115
Scottish Cup	42	1	25
League Cup	62	1	38
Europe	40	1	10
Total	**377**	**6**	**188**

14 | MADE IN PARADISE

FAMOUS FIVE

No.1 - A bright future...

In the dark and distant days of the year 1888, the news pretty much reflected our modern-day thoughts of life in the rain-soaked cobbled streets and alleys of Victorian Britain.

Jack The Ripper had sliced up five women in London but in those early days he had yet to be christened with the bloodcurdling moniker - he was simply known as the Whitechapel Murderer.

Land League rebellion in Ireland and crofters' riots in Scotland's Western Isles also kept the Peelers and other law enforcement divisions busy.

Kaiser Wilhelm II became Emperor of Germany, the *Financial Times* was first published and in Glasgow there was the International Exhibition of Industry, Science and Art held in the affluent West End.

Across the Big Pond, Benjamin Harrison was elected the 23rd US President by ousting Grover Cleveland in the November 6 election.

Exactly 12 months earlier on November 6, 1887 a rather more important voting process was taking place in the East End of Glasgow at St Mary's Hall in the Calton's East Rose Street.

Brother Walfrid of the Marist Order had convened a meeting of local Irish businessmen to organise the foundation of a football team to raise money for charity - and the rest, as they day, is history.

That history though, was ensured by the first committee's determination that this new club would not be a fly-by-night operation and, although within a week they had leased six acres of land beside the Eastern Necropolis, they had resolved to show patience and guarantee the Celtic Football Club would be run as proper going concern.

For every club that blossomed, though, there were dozens that floundered and by not jumping in at the deep end right away, the club's founders ensured that the new Celtic team would flourish.

Indeed, it would be seven months before this new side would kick a ball in earnest for the first time and, as fate would have it, Celtic kicked off their footballing history against a team from the other side of the city called Rangers.

It was on May 28, 1888 that a crowd of 2,000 braved a chilly evening to watch this new team take on the established side from the South Side at the first Celtic Park.

The Celts took to the field in their original outfits of white shirts with green collars with a red and green Celtic cross on the breast as they recorded a win in their first ever game against a side who were to become their greatest rivals.

The game was won 5-2 with the honour of scoring Celtic's first ever goal falling to Neil McCallum who, just nine months later, would also score Celtic's first Scottish Cup final goal.

The Scottish Umpire of the day said that Celtic played with: "a combination which could scarcely have been expected from an opening display.

"It would appear that the newly-formed Glasgow club, the Celtic FC, has a bright future before it. At any rate, if the committee can place the same eleven on the field as opposed Rangers last Monday evening, or an equally strong one, the Celtic will not lack for patronage or support."

They certainly got that right and it's thought that the 2,000 attendance could have been greater but for the International Exhibition taking place the same day through in the West End.

The only surviving remnant of the 1888 International Exhibition is the Doulton Fountain, the world's largest terracotta fountain and it now takes pride of place outside the People's Palace in Glasgow's East End...

We like to think that a rather more authentic, focal and indeed international legacy of 1888's Industry, Science and Art Exhibition still survives today just along the road a little deeper inside the East End.

STORY OF OUR LEGENDS

STEVIE CHALMERS

1959 - 1971

Stevie Chalmers scored 231 goals for Celtic during a 12-year career with the club, making him the fourth top goalscorer of all-time. Only Henrik Larsson (242), Bobby Lennox (277) and Jimmy McGrory (468) have scored more goals for Celtic. Yet that trio of legends can't claim to have score the single most important goal in Celtic's history. Stevie Chalmers can. It came on Thursday, May 25, 1967 at the Estadio Nacional in Lisbon.

With just five minutes of the European Cup final remaining, Chalmers knocked home a Bobby Murdoch shot into the Inter Milan net to give Celtic a 2-1 victory and ensured they became the first club from Northern Europe to lift the prestigious trophy.

If Lisbon was the pinnacle, then there were many other highlights for the forward who had made his debut as far back as 1959. He netted a league hat-trick against Rangers, the last Celt to do so up to 2014; only Bobby Lennox in the Glasgow Cup and Harry Hood in the League Cup have matched that feat. Chalmers also scored in the 1969 Scottish Cup final, hit five goals in a game against Hamilton Accies, when Lennox also scored five that night, and was top scorer in four seasons.

Like so many that had come before him, Stevie Chalmers' pathway to Paradise came via the Garngad. As the area had produced the great Jimmy McGrory, Chalmers had a lot to live up to but soon caught the eye of Celtic after a fruitful junior career during which he turned out for the likes of Kirkintilloch Rob Roy and Ashfield.

And his first steps on the road to becoming a Celtic legend were influenced by father, David, who was his idol. Having started his career at Celtic but not made a first-team appearance, David Chalmers would go on to turn out for Clydebank. It was during this time that he would take to the field alongside Jimmy McGrory, who was on loan at the club, allowing the young Chalmers to be brought up with countless stories about the skills of the Celtic legend.

His arrival at Celtic in the February of 1959 coincided with the emergence of youngsters such as Billy McNeill and John Clark who would soon be joined by the likes of Jimmy Johnstone, John Hughes and Tommy Gemmell, a group who were given the moniker of the Kelly Kids after the then Celtic chairman Robert Kelly, and would form the spine of Celtic's most successful ever team.

The absolute highlight for Stevie Chalmers, along with his team-mates, came on May 25, 1967, with the European Cup triumph in Lisbon. He won a total of 15 trophies with Celtic, and was in the team which lifted the Scottish Cup in 1965, the club's first trophy under Jock Stein. He scored 231 goals for the club, and he was the last Celt to net a league hat-trick against Rangers, the treble coming on January 3, 1966 in a 5-1 derby demolition. He was also part of the Celtic team which swept their Glasgow rivals aside in the 1969 Scottish Cup final to secure a domestic treble. Yet, for the striker, it always comes right back to Lisbon and that goal.

STEVIE CHALMERS

FORWARD
Celtic debut: March 10, 1959, League, Celtic 1-2 Airdrie

	App	Subs	Goals
League	253	8	158
Scottish Cup	45	2	33
League Cup	57	2	27
Europe	38	1	13
Total	**393**	**13**	**231**

16 | MADE IN PARADISE

Chalmers won a total of 15 trophies with Celtic, and was in the team which lifted the Scottish Cup in 1965, the club's first trophy under Jock Stein

STORY OF OUR LEGENDS

BOBBY MURDOCH

1959 - 1973

'When Bobby Murdoch played, Celtic played.' That is the collective agreement among his Celtic team-mates, and in a team bursting at the seams with world-class talent, there can be no greater accolade than that. Murdoch was central to Celtic's success under Jock Stein, developing a midfield partnership with Bertie Auld that was the envy of the football world.

Murdoch played nearly 500 games for Celtic and scored 102 goals. He could have played more, and scored more, were it not for the ankle injury that sometimes meant an enforced absence from the team, or the fact that he was allowed to leave the club in 1973 for Middlesbrough.

Celtic's legendary manager, Jock Stein said: 'As far as I am concerned, Bobby Murdoch was just about the best player I had as manager. I only let him move because he had run out of challenges with Celtic,' while Inter Milan manager, Helenio Herrera, described Bobby Murdoch as 'my complete player'.

Although raised in Rutherglen, within walking distance of a match at Celtic Park, boundary rules meant that

> **Murdoch was central to Celtic's success under Jock Stein, developing a midfield partnership with Bertie Auld that was the envy of the football world**

Bobby Murdoch travelled deeper into Lanarkshire for secondary schooling and, like Billy McNeill, played for Our Lady's High in Motherwell. Indeed, he did have a trial for Motherwell but once Celtic came calling, there was no doubt where he would end up. He signed for his Bhoyhood heroes on October 23, 1959 and the youngster was farmed out to Cambuslang Rangers.

Celtic's 1962/63 season kicked off with a home League Cup tie against Hearts on August 11. The legend goes that 22-year-old John Divers forgot his boots and the re-shuffled side saw the just-turned 18-year-old Bobby Murdoch drafted into the side at the last minute, although it is also claimed that he was always going to be playing that day and it was, in fact, Charlie Gallagher, who was drafted in to replace Divers. Either way, both players would score, with the Celtic debutant netting the first of his 102 goals for the club just seven minutes into the game. Gallagher added a second and John Hughes completed the scoring.

Murdoch would go on to win eight of the nine-in-a-row championships as well as four Scottish Cups and five consecutive League Cups. Then, of course, there was the European Cup in 1967

to make for a haul of no fewer than 18 top-level medals.

His last game in the Hoops came in the final sectional game of the League Cup on August 29, 1973 away to Arbroath when Celtic won 3-1. Just a few weeks later, one of the greatest footballers Celtic had ever produced was on his way out of Paradise and moving down to Ayresome Park and Middlesbrough.

However, Bobby Murdoch always remained a Celt, a supporter first and foremost, who was one of the finest players ever to grace the green and white Hoops. He was gone from us far too soon, passing away at the age of 56 on May 15, 2001.

BOBBY MURDOCH

MIDFIELDER
Celtic debut: August 11, 1962, League Cup, Celtic 3-1 Hearts (scored once)

	App	Subs	Goals
League	287	4	61
Scottish Cup	84	0	17
League Cup	53	0	13
Europe	57	0	11
Total	**481**	**4**	**102**

18 | MADE IN PARADISE

BOBBY MURDOCH

NEILLY MOCHAN
1953 - 1960

There aren't many players who win two trophies in front of combined crowds of almost 300,000 supporters before making their 'official' first-team debut. But the late, great Neil Mochan enjoyed that particular honour.

Outside-left, 'Neilly' joined Celtic on May 8, 1953 after three successful years spent on Teeside with Middlesbrough and the following day, made his Hoops debut in the Glasgow Charity Cup final against Queen's Park.

Just as he had made an immediate impact after his transfer to England from Morton (scoring in a 2-1 debut win over Tottenham), Mochan did the same on his return to Scotland, bagging two goals in that 3-1 cup final victory.

Arriving at the tail-end of a disappointing season, where Celtic had finished eighth in a 16-team top flight, there was little that the then-26-year-old could do to influence league matters.

But the supporters were given a further glimpse of the forward's talent, eye for goal and irrepressible character as Celtic concluded the season with their involvement in that year's Coronation Cup.

Few had given Celtic a chance going into this competition against the cream of the British leagues, but in their first match against favourites Arsenal they handed the English champions a footballing lesson, with Bobby Collins scoring the only goal in a game dominated by the Scots.

In their next game Celtic faced the English runners-up, Manchester United and this time it was Mochan's strike which earned the 2-1 win and Celtic's place in the final against league runners-up, Hibs.

Mochan's magnificent 35-yarder (struck with his weaker right foot) got Celtic off the mark in the Hampden final and Jimmy Walsh grabbed Celtic's second, but with the competition not recognised as 'competitive' outings Neilly was still looking forward to his competitive debut when season 1953/54 kicked off in August.

The subsequent season he played his part in the team's league and Scottish Cup double success, while one of his, and Celtic's finest hours of the decade came in October 1957 when he scored twice in the 7-1 rout of Rangers in the League Cup final.

Those achievements were impressive enough, but Neilly Mochan's contribution to the Celtic story didn't stop in 1960. He returned to the club in February 1964 as a coach, and he would remain at Paradise until his untimely death in 1994.

He was part of Jock Stein's backroom staff and played a key role with Stein and another former team-mate, Sean Fallon, in delivering unprecedented success to the club, most notably on May 25, 1967 when Celtic beat Inter Milan 2-1 in Lisbon to win the European Cup.

As Jock Stein's trainer, Mochan prepared the Lions for that final victory over Inter Milan and three years later, he again led the team  for training before the European Cup final against Feyenoord.

It was a role he served under successive Celtic managers until 1991 when he took up the position of kit manager, but continued to lend his invaluable experience to generation after generation of young players.

Established stars, from Bertie Auld and Billy McNeill in the 1960s to Paul McStay and Peter Grant in the '80s and '90s, spoke of Mochan's influence and he was the heartbeat of the dressing-room until he sadly passed away in 1994 after a brave fight against leukaemia.

NEILLY MOCHAN
OUTSIDE-LEFT
Celtic debut: August 8, 1953; League Cup, Celtic 0-1 Aberdeen

	App	Subs	Goals
League	191	n/a	81
Scottish Cup	34	n/a	16
League Cup	43	n/a	12
Europe	n/a	n/a	n/a
Total	**268**	**n/a**	**109**

JOHN FALLON

1958 - 1972

When John Fallon joined Celtic on December 11, 1958, he fulfilled a lifelong dream, signing for the club he had supported passionately as a boy.

He joined as an 18-year-old and was farmed out to Fauldhouse United and made the breakthrough from Jock Stein's coaching system when regular keeper Frank Haffey was injured at work.

Fallon made his debut for the first team in a league game against Clyde at Celtic Park on September, 26, 1959 shortly after his 19th birthday.

Following that, he made fleeting appearances while Haffey held the gloves but by November, 1963 he had made the No.1 spot his own until the arrival of Ronnie Simpson.

The Blantyre-born goalkeeper was understudy to Ronnie Simpson in the all-conquering season of 1966/67 and was one of the first on the pitch at Lisbon to celebrate when the final whistle sounded.

Fallon later took over from Simpson and went on to play 184 first team games, in many ways epitomising the passion and enthusiasm of the Celtic support.

Among his greatest performances was an inspirational display in a 0-0 draw with AC Milan at the San Siro in 1969 amid a heavy blizzard and also in the victory over Real Madrid in Alfredo Di Stefano's Testimonial two years previously.

Fallon is also credited with a leading role in the 1969 League Cup final win over St Johnstone, with some commentators stating that his two saves near the end of the game effectively handed Celtic the cup.

John Fallon grew up listening to songs and stories of John Thomson's greatness, and it was a dream come true, as a supporter, to become a Celtic goalkeeper himself and, indeed, he was one of a select band of only a handful of Celts such as Billy McNeill, John Clark and Stevie Chalmers to play with the Hoops in the 1950s, all the way through the 1960s to the 1970s.

And, it is fitting that he played just as an important part in introducing the success-strewn and trophy-laden golden years of Celtic as Billy McNeill.

Everyone knows that it was big Cesar who rose to head home the winner in the Hoops' tide-changing 3-2 Scottish Cup final win over Dunfermline Athletic in 1965.

What has become lost in the green mists of time, though, is that John Fallon produced two excellent save to stop the Fife team from taking the lead for a third time - our history could have been very different if either of those attempts had gone in.

He was also presented by his team-mates to the crowd at the end of the 1969 Scottish Cup final 4-0 win over Rangers when some excellent saves contributed a clean sheet to a magnificent overall team performance.

He was also Celtic 12th man that historic night in Lisbon as in the pre-substitute days a back-up keeper was allowed on the bench for the first time in a European Cup final.

And as the 12th man term had become synonymous with devoted and unfaltering backing of the men on the pitch, it's more than appropriate that the man on the bench that night would bleed green and white if you cut him.

If John Fallon had been in the employ of any other club he would still have been in Lisbon that night on the terraces wearing a Celtic scarf rather than on the bench wearing a keeper's top.

JOHN FALLON

GOALKEEPER
Celtic debut:
September 26, 1959,
League,
Celtic 1-1 Clyde

	App	Subs	Goals
League	125	0	0
Scottish Cup	14	0	0
League Cup	36	0	0
Europe	20	0	0
Total	**195**	**0**	**0**

STORY OF OUR LEGENDS

JIMMY McGRORY
1922 - 1937

Born in the Hoops stronghold of Garngad, there was little doubt as to where the heart of young James Edward McGrory lay.

That, however, could be said for most of most residents of the area but it would seem that this youngster was destined to live the dream. If Celtic weren't in action, most fans in the area would walk along to Provanmill Park to watch the recently-formed St Roch's Juniors where Jimmy McGrory played as a 16-year-old.

However, it wasn't long before the seniors had their eye on the striker but, despite a trial for Bury, it was no surprise when the teenager signed on the dotted line for his beloved Celtic.

He is, without question, the greatest goalscorer ever to have played for Celtic. McGrory scored a phenomenal 468 goals during a 15-year career with the club, averaging more than a goal a game.

This was also in an era before the League Cup or European football, so McGrory's tally from 445 games is even more remarkable. However, it almost does a disservice to only refer to him as Celtic's top scorer of all-time because McGrory is the greatest goalscorer in the history of British football.

JIMMY McGRORY
CENTRE-FORWARD
Celtic debut:
January 20, 1923,
League,
Third Lanark 1-0 Celtic

	App	Subs	Goals
League	378	n/a	395
Scottish Cup	67	n/a	73
League Cup	n/a	n/a	n/a
Europe	n/a	n/a	n/a
Total	**445**	**n/a**	**468**

22 | Made In Paradise

JIMMY McGRORY

In 11 different matches, he netted four goals, and he produced an incredible THIRTY-NINE hat-tricks during the 15 years he played for his beloved green and white Hoops

Season 1923/24 saw him loaned out to Clydebank where, under the leadership of former Celt, Jimmy 'Dun' Hay, he began to blossom as a centre-forward, scoring 23 goals for the Bankies that season including one against the Hoops at Celtic Park on March 4, 1924 when Clydebank won 2-1. It was, McGrory later said, 'the goal that reminded Celtic I existed.'

When he returned to Celtic, he launched a goalscoring career that remains without parallel. Even just a cursory glance at the history books can almost take the breath away. Jimmy McGrory scored five goals in a single game on no fewer than four occasions. In 11 different matches, he netted four goals, and he produced an incredible **THIRTY-NINE** hat-tricks during the 15 years he played for his beloved green and white Hoops.

In 12 of the 13 seasons he played when he returned to the club in 1924 after his loan spell with Clydebank, he was the club's top goalscorer, breaking all previous scoring records and setting new ones that would never be broken.

He was also twice Europe's leading goalscorer – in 1926/27 (49 goals) and 1935/36 (50 goals) – and as well as all the singles, doubles, trebles, quadruples and quintuples he scored, on January 14, 1928, he scored **EIGHT** goals in a 9-0 victory over Dunfermline Athletic.

He won league championship badges in 1926 and 1936 and Scottish Cup medals in 1925, 1927, 1931, 1933 and 1937.

The 1925 Scottish Cup final will forever be known as 'The Patsy Gallacher Final' for the Irishman's acrobatics to score Celtic's equaliser, but it was McGrory's header with three minutes of the match remaining which won the cup for the Hoops.

And like every player of that generation, whatever highs that might have been achieved were overshadowed by the most terrible of lows, and Jimmy McGrory, along with his Celtic team-mates, was left devastated by the tragic death of goalkeeper John Thomson on September 5, 1931.

As a goalscorer, Jimmy McGrory remains peerless, and he's certainly the greatest ever to have worn the famous green and white Hoops.

STORY OF OUR LEGENDS

JIM CRAIG
1965 - 1972

He was the last of the Lisbon Lions to come through the ranks at Celtic Park and, in line with that, apart from the incoming Willie Wallace a year later, he was the last to make his debut.

Befitting a Lion, this young right-back made his debut in a European match as he took part in the Hoops' 1-0 win over Dutch side Go Ahead Deventer in the European Cup-Winners' Cup on October 10, 1965.

The name of the opposition, Go Ahead Deventer, proved to be prophetic as the youngster did indeed go ahead and make the right-back berth his own amid some startling competition for places

The name of the opposition side proved to be prophetic as the youngster did indeed go ahead and make the right-back berth his own amid some startling competition for places in a side that would have the choice of a remarkable conveyor belt of talent over the following years.

For seven years he was a first-team Celt and there is no doubt that the highlight of his career came less than two years after his debut when he travelled with the rest of the squad to Lisbon and returned with the European Cup.

Personally, he was involved in two big turning points in the game when he was adjudged to have given away the penalty that Inter Milan took their early lead from.

However, if any atonement was needed, he produced it in spades when, on one of his foraging runs down the right flank, he cut the ball back for fellow full-back Tommy Gemmell who cannonballed a shot into the net for the equaliser.

The rest, as they say, is part of Celtic's rich and illustrious history and he was to go on write himself into another chapter in the annals of the club when he joined a rather elite club.

That was because his final game as a Celt was the Scottish Cup final of May 6, 1972 when the Hoops beat Hibernian 6-1 and he joined that band of players who went out on a high with a trophy win on their final day.

JIM CRAIG
RIGHT-BACK
Celtic debut:
October 10, 1965,
European Cup-Winners' Cup,
Celtic 1-0 Go Ahead Deventer

	App	Subs	Goals
League	143	4	1
Scottish Cup	21	2	0
League Cup	29	1	4
Europe	31	0	1
Total	**224**	**7**	**6**

JIM CRAIG

However, that was the last of a raft of winner's medals with the Hoops who he joined as an amateur from Glasgow University AC where he played football while studying to become a dentist.

Aside from the European Cup, the full-back also lifted seven league titles, four Scottish Cups and three League Cups in a seven-year period for a total of 15 top-level trophies with two Glasgow Cup medals added for good measure.

He missed out on the 1966 tour of Bermuda and North America due to his finals at Glasgow University and therefore had to fight to earn his place in the team ahead of Willie O'Neill, but by halfway through the glorious season of 1966/67 he had made the right-back berth his own.

It was there that he operated in tandem with Tommy Gemmell on the left, a partnership that was to prove priceless in the final competitive game of that season.

He was also a figurehead in the run-up to Fergus McCann's takeover in 1994 and worked regularly as a media pundit with the club in the years following.

STORY OF OUR LEGENDS

BOBBY LENNOX

1961 - 1978, 1978 - 1980

The late, great Alfredo Di Stefano, recalling his testimonial match at the Bernabeu Stadium in 1967, when the newly-crowned European champions beat Real Madrid 1-0 courtesy of a Bobby Lennox goal, said: 'The Scotsman who gave me the most trouble was Bobby Lennox of Celtic. My testimonial at the Bernabeu was against Celtic as, of course, they were the champions of Europe in 1967. And although I remember the Bernabeu rising to Jimmy Johnstone, I admired Lennox greatly.'

And Manchester United legend, Bobby Charlton, put it simply: 'If I'd had Bobby Lennox in my team, I could have played forever.'

Lennox was the 'foreigner' in the Lisbon Lions squad, living the furthest from Celtic Park – a full 30 miles away in Saltcoats. He played secondary school football with St Michael's in Irvine before, in 1959, turning out with Star of the Sea Amateurs and Ardeer Recreation.

He was already starting to catch the eye and when his beloved Celtic showed interest, there was only ever going to be one outcome. Barely a week after his 18th birthday, he signed for Celtic on September 5, 1961.

The winger was still only 18 when he made his Celtic debut when top-of-the-table Dundee visited on league duty on March 3, 1962. A 39,000 crowd converged on Celtic Park for the game but, surprisingly, for a player whose speed would be renowned throughout the world, it was reported that the pace of the game found him wanting. The visitors took the lead early in the second-half before two late Celtic goals gave the Hoops a 2-1 win against a side that would go on to win the title that season.

There were fleeting appearances over the next few seasons but it wasn't until the second half of the 1964/65 season that Lennox became a regular in the side – and that co-incided with the trophies rolling in at Celtic Park on a green and white conveyor belt. The medals came thick and fast for Lennox from then on in, with no fewer than 11 championship gongs, eight Scottish Cups and four League Cups as well as, of course, the European Cup in 1967. A total of 24 top-class

> **A total of 24 top-class medals were won by Lennox in a career that spanned the greatest years in the club's history**

medals were won by Lennox in a career that spanned the greatest years in the club's history.

There were two farewells to Paradise for Bobby Lennox. On November 16, 1977, Celtic played St Mirren in the second-leg of the League Cup quarter-final and were 3-1 up from the first game at Love Street. The 17,000 crowd saw Celtic win 2-0 thanks to goals from Paul Wilson and Johnny Doyle, and it was Doyle who Lennox replaced from the bench. That was his last game before joining Houston Hurricane on March 29, 1978 but his spell Stateside was short-lived as in September of the same year, new Celtic manager, Billy McNeill, called him back for another term. His final game was the Scottish Cup final of 1980 when he again replaced Johnny Doyle in a 1-0 win over Rangers thanks to George McCluskey's goal.

Bobby Lennox scored an impressive 277 goals for Celtic, making him Celtic's second top goalscorer of all-time. It was always going to be a nigh-on impossible task to get anywhere near Jimmy McGrory's record of 468 goals, although the Lisbon Lion would have got considerably closer if it hadn't been for the regular intervention of the linesman's flag.

BOBBY LENNOX

OUTSIDE-LEFT
Celtic debut:
March 3, 1962
League,
Celtic 2-1 Dundee

	App	Subs	Goals
League	297	49	170
Scottish Cup	46	5	31
League Cup	107	13	62
Europe	57	12	14
Total	**507**	**79**	**277**

BOBBY LENNOX

STORY OF OUR LEGENDS

PAT BONNER
1978 - 1997

Donegal Bhoy, Pat Bonner played GAA with Rosses Rovers, but he began his association football career with local club Keadue Rovers, a well-respected junior side in the county and that led to a trial with Leicester City in season 1975/76. His performances there soon caught the eye of Celtic's supreme talent spotter and fellow Irishman, Sean Fallon, and in May 1978, he became Jock Stein's last signing for the club. It was to prove to be another excellent acquisition by Celtic's greatest ever manager.

Fittingly, Pat Bonner made his Celtic debut on St Patrick's Day in a 2-1 home win over Motherwell in 1979. However, his real breakthrough is credited as occurring in the following year during Danny McGrain's testimonial game against Manchester United. After regular shot-stopper, Peter Latchford, suffered a hand injury, the young Irishman was elevated to the starting line-up for the prestigious encounter. He grasped the opportunity with both hands. The fixture finished 0-0 and the keeper produced an impressive performance, and he never looked back after that.

When you make over 600 appearances for Celtic, winning trophies would seem a natural outcome. And that was certainly the case with Packie, particularly during the early part of his career. He was instrumental in the championship victories of 1981, 1982, 1986 and 1988, and won three Scottish Cups in 1985, 1989 and 1995 – a back injury kept him out of the 1988 triumph. His solitary League Cup success, secured in 1982, meant he won every domestic honour as a Celtic player.

Lou Macari released him at the end of the 1993/94 season, seeming to spell an end of a long and illustrious association with the club. Former team-mate Tommy Burns took him to Kilmarnock but when he replaced Macari as manager later on that summer, he brought Packie back home as player/coach.

That Indian Summer resulting from the intervention of Burns delivered another 25 appearances for the keeper that not only brought him up level with Alec McNair in the appearance charts, but also presented him with the opportunity to go out on a high.

It restarted for real on Boxing Day, 1995 when he took over the No.1 position from Gordon Marshall. He maintained his place for every single game except the Scottish Cup fourth-round win over Meadowbank Thistle.

This meant he was between the sticks for the final on May 27 when a Pierre van Hooijdonk goal against Airdrie delivered Celtic's first silverware since 1999. It was the perfect way to bow out as a Celt, helping to win a trophy for his manager and friend, Tommy Burns.

There will always be one moment which will define Pat Bonner's career and it came in the penalty-shoot out in the Republic of Ireland's victory over Romania at Italia '90. With the scores tied, he saved Daniel Timofte's effort which allowed David O'Leary the chance to send Ireland through to the last eight of the competition.

However, in his 253 clean sheets for Celtic, and thousands of saves along the way in 641 appearances, his favourite save is rather less well-known for it was stopping a free-kick from former-Celt Andy Ritchie of Morton down at Greenock.

He's also a national hero – a treasure even – for his heroics in 80 appearances for the Republic of Ireland, particularly in that 1990 World Cup in Italy. Indeed, in 2002, he was given the rare honour of appearing on an Irish postage stamp.

PAT BONNER
GOALKEEPER
Celtic debut:
March 17, 1979,
League,
Celtic 2-1 Motherwell

	App	Subs	Goals
League	483	0	0
Scottish Cup	55	0	0
League Cup	64	0	0
Europe	39	0	0
Total	**641**	**0**	**0**

ROY AITKEN

1982 - 1997

Roy Aitken was 75 days short of his 17th birthday when he made the first of 672 appearances for Celtic in September 1975. He might only have been a teenager but Roy Aitken was always a man, a strong, fearless and imposing character, with an incredible will to win that did, on more than one occasion, snatch victory from the jaws of defeat. While he would only make three appearances in his first season, the next season he was an established first-team player and would remain so until he left in 1990.

He began life in midfield, a combative presence in a team that was still adjusting to life without Davie Hay, who had departed for Chelsea, but as his career progressed, he took a step back into the heart of the defence

Aitken was fortunate enough to play with three generations of Celtic greats – Bobby Lennox from the Lions era, Kenny Dalglish and Danny McGrain from the Quality Street Gang, and then contemporaries like Tommy Burns and later Paul McStay. Aitken could stand shoulder to shoulder with any of these men as a legend of the club, and he played a pivotal role in many Celtic successes in the 1970s and '80s.

There were doubles in 1977 and 1988, of which the latter was particularly special, given that it was Celtic's centenary season and Roy Aitken was the captain, while the title success in 1986 was also memorable.

Yet, there are two games which stick out as great triumphs and perfect examples of just what Aitken brought to the team.

There was the 1985 Scottish Cup triumph, when he grabbed the Celtic team by the scruff of the neck when they were trailing 1-0 to Dundee United and hauled them back into the game. Davie Provan and Frank McGarvey scored the goals to win the 100th Scottish Cup final, the latter heading home an Aitken cross. And then there was the night that '10 men won the league'.

That 1979 triumph truly was the stuff of legend. Celtic needed to beat Rangers to win the title, and when they found themselves trailing 1-0 and reduced to 10 men following Johnny Doyle's dismissal, it looked like an impossible task. Yet Aitken, along with a team of inspirational characters all wearing green and white-Hooped jerseys, refused to accept defeat and eventually ran out 4-2 winners to become Scottish champions. Indeed, it was his goal on 66 minutes which was Celtic's first of the night, and drew the team level, though there were to be many more twists and turns before the final whistle sounded and Celtic were confirmed as league winners once again.

He took over as Celtic captain in 1987, succeeding Danny McGrain, who had left the club in the summer. It was an important season for the new skipper, given that Celtic were celebrating their centenary, and with Billy McNeill back in charge of the team, it was the perfect double act to deliver success is such an important year.

After 672 games for Celtic, 'The Bear' was leaving Paradise, moving south to join Newcastle United. There have been many great players who've walked through 'Parkhead's gates', including Roy Aitken, but few could match his determination and dedication to the cause.

ROY AITKEN

MIDFIELDER
Celtic debut:
April 4, 1984,
League,
Rangers 1-0 Celtic

	App	Subs	Goals
League	483	0	40
Scottish Cup	55	0	2
League Cup	82	2	6
Europe	50	0	4
Total	670	2	52

STORY OF OUR LEGENDS

CHRIS SUTTON
2000 - 2006

Chris Sutton was one of the first signings of Martin O'Neill's Celtic revolution and he proved an instant hit with the Hoops faithful.

The big striker joined in a big-money move from Chelsea where he had failed to find his feet after becoming one of England's most feared frontmen at Blackburn, a team he had memorably helped to the English Premier League title in 1995.

Martin O'Neill was confident Sutton would soon rediscover his best form in Paradise and justify his high price tag and the Irishman, not for the first time, was proved correct as Sutton made a sensational start in the Hoops.

A goal on his debut in a 2-1 win at Tannadice was quickly followed up by a double in a 6-2 humiliation of Rangers – coined the 'Demolition Derby' – earning him hero-status among the Hoops faithful. Celtic were on the rise again and Sutton was one of the main reasons for the resurgence.

Powerful, formidable in the air yet technical, he proved a perfect foil for Henrik Larsson up front and they terrorised defences across the country as a rampant Celtic swept all before them on their way to a first domestic treble in 32 years.

Significantly, Sutton was also a strong character, a winner, and he fitted in seamlessly into a dressing room where the desire for success and resolve were legendary. Nothing fazed him.

He and his Celtic colleagues would lift further silverware in his second season at the club as a second title was secured by a huge margin, the Hoops only suffering one defeat throughout the entire campaign.

This was also the term in which the Bhoys secured passage to the UEFA Champions League group stages for the first time, with Sutton bagging a number of crucial goals during the European adventure, including a spectacular winner in the thrilling 4-3 home victory over Juventus.

John Hartson's arrival saw Sutton's valuable versatility come to the fore. To allow Hartson to team up with Larsson in attack, the Englishman was frequently deployed in a deeper role, usually in midfield but also in central defence. His all-round ability meant he coped with these positional switches with consummate ease.

Nevertheless, Sutton was still able to contribute in the scoring department and he was only one goal shy of 20 in the 2002/03 campaign as Celtic sensationally reached the UEFA Cup final in Seville only to suffer the agony of the extra-time defeat to Porto.

His next season would be his most prolific for the club. The hit-man bagged 28 goals in all competitions as the Hoops romped to the championship, winning 25 successive games in the process – a new Scottish record.

Towards the end of this season, he scored one of his most memorable goals for the club. In the dying seconds of the Glasgow derby, he out-muscled Frank de Boer outside the box before sending a sublime chip into the top corner. Paradise erupted as Celtic secured the victory that completed the 'whitewash' of five wins over the Ibrox side.

This mixture of strength, skill and an aptitude for delivering on the big occasion were all typical Sutton and he continued to be a key player in O'Neill's final season which provided him with another Scottish Cup medal. However, losing the league title on the last day of the season for the second time in three years meant it was an ultimately disappointing campaign for both player and club.

Just over six months later, Sutton exited Paradise to sign for Birmingham City, his place secure as a Celtic great.

CHRIS SUTTON

FORWARD
Celtic debut:
July 31, 2000,
League Cup,
Dundee United 1-2 Celtic
(scored once)

	App	Subs	Goals
League	127	3	60
Scottish Cup	16	0	5
League Cup	8	1	2
Europe	41	2	16
Total	**192**	**6**	**83**

SANDY McMAHON
1890 - 1903

In the pantheon of Celtic greats, the name of Alexander McMahon must rank alongside some of the more illustrious or well-known names that immediately spring to mind.

Indeed, it could be argued that McMahon, better known as Sandy, and often eulogised by supporters of the time as 'the Duke', was the very first legend of the club. Certainly, he was the first player to pass the 100-goal mark and for that alone he deserves to be recognised.

He also stands at the head of a great goalscoring lineage which has stretched down through Celtic's history. After McMahon came Jimmy Quinn, then Patsy Gallacher and Jimmy McGrory in the pre-Second World War era, to be followed later by the likes of Bobby Lennox, Stevie Chalmers, Kenny Dalglish and Henrik Larsson.

That his Celtic career spanned the late 19th and early 20th centuries is one factor why his name and exports are not as widely known or celebrated as they should be, but the history books have recorded the 177 goals he scored for Celtic in 217 appearances and that marks him out as a special talent as well

as being the eighth top goalscorer in the club's history.

McMahon was an integral part of Celtic's first trophy successes, with the Scottish Cup win of 1892 followed a year later by the club's very first league championship. He was a goalscorer, but also a dribbler in the finest Celtic traditions.

It was him, along with the likes of Johnny Campbell and Johnny Madden, who provided entertainment and artistry to football and the Celtic team in particular, beginning a tradition of playing football that has evolved down through the years and has become known as 'the Celtic way'.

He scored the first of his 177 goals on April 11, 1891, securing a 1-0 victory for the Bhoys at home to Dumbarton. His final goal for the club came on February 14, 1902 in a first round Scottish Cup tie against St Mirren. He was one of four scorers that day in a 4-0 victory for the Celts, though it was a second replay of the tie, the two previous games having finished 0-0 and 1-1. He netted Celtic's third of the game.

Two weeks after scoring that goal, McMahon played his final game for the club, in a Scottish Cup quarter-final tie against Rangers at Celtic Park. Sadly, he wasn't able to bow out with a goal.

While Sandy McMahon remained at the club until October 1903 when he joined Partick Thistle, one of the greatest players Celtic has ever produced never wore the famous green and white Hoops in a competitive game. He had only played in the green and white stripes. Celtic changed their strip to the Hoops at the start of season 1903/04 but McMahon had already played his last game for the club.

Sandy McMahon was still a relatively young man when he passed away in 1916 – he was only 45-years-old – but he had ensured a lasting place in the annals of Celtic history. He was, and remains, a true Celtic great. He won't be the last but he was probably the first.

> **Sandy McMahon stands at the head of a great goalscoring lineage which has stretched down through Celtic's history**

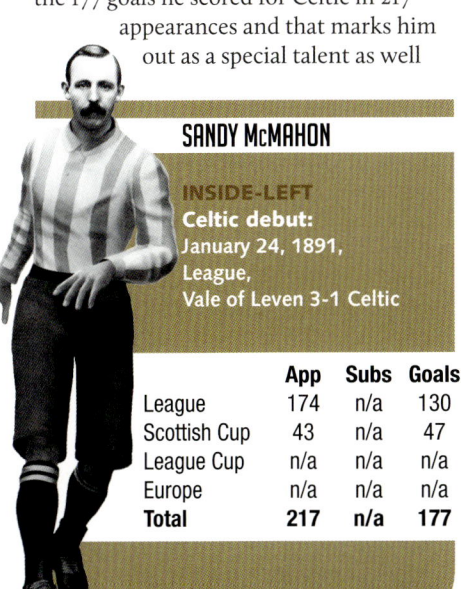

SANDY McMAHON

INSIDE-LEFT
Celtic debut:
January 24, 1891,
League,
Vale of Leven 3-1 Celtic

	App	Subs	Goals
League	174	n/a	130
Scottish Cup	43	n/a	47
League Cup	n/a	n/a	n/a
Europe	n/a	n/a	n/a
Total	217	n/a	177

STORY OF OUR LEGENDS

STILIYAN PETROV
1999 - 2006

Stiliyan Petrov arrived in Glasgow a talented and precocious young player in 1999 but left seven years later a leader of men and one of the club's most loved midfielders.

Signed by John Barnes from CSKA Sofia at the age of just 19, Bulgarian Petrov carved out a positive reputation in an overall disappointing season for the Celts and went on to become one of the key pillars of the success built at the club under Martin O'Neill when he took over in 2000.

Petrov was initially deployed at right-back for the Hoops and made his debut there in a 2-1 loss to Dundee United, but his key attributes of strength and vision, combined with his dynamic forward play, made him more suited to a midfield role and it was there he excelled after being moved to the centre of the pitch by O'Neill.

In the Irishman's first season, Petrov was a mainstay of the treble-winning team, operating at the top of a midfield triangle completed by Paul Lambert and Neil Lennon and he notched eight goals in 37 appearances across all competitions.

His swashbuckling approach to attack and defence made him an instant hit with the Celtic fans, as did his three goals in the opening six games of the season, one of which came in the 6-2 demolition derby against Rangers.

By Petrov's third season at the club he was a true fans' favourite and played regularly as the team made it to the final of the UEFA Cup in Seville in 2003, scoring against VfB Stuttgart in a 3-1 home win in the fourth round.

His link-up play was crucial to the prolific partnership of Henrik Larsson and Chris Sutton over this time and although the Celts ultimately finished that season empty-handed, Petrov's stock had risen considerably at club and international level.

He continued to excel in Glasgow in O'Neill's final season in 2004/05, winning the Celtic Player of the Year Award and the Scottish Cup, and he remained a key component of the side under new manager Gordon Strachan in the 2005/06 season.

In the summer of 2006 Petrov completed a transfer to Aston Villa in the English Premier League to rejoin O'Neill after amassing a total of 10 trophies at Celtic and he was eventually made captain of the Birmingham-based club.

In 2013 he was forced to retire from playing football after a battle with leukaemia, having being diagnosed the year before. Support for the former midfielder was unwavering from the Celtic family, however, and he returned to the club frequently during his recovery to thank the fans for their backing.

The culmination of this support came in September, 2013 when a charity match was organised at Celtic Park featuring a Celtic and Stiliyan XI, allowing Petrov to play in front of the fans once more at Paradise.

Still very much in the depths of his recovery at the time, Petrov only played a few minutes in the game but the lasting image from that day will be of the Bulgarian with tears in his eyes as he embraced his family in front of the packed stadium in awe of the turnout on a memorable afternoon.

The emotion of that event encapsulated the mutual love shared between the fans and the Hoops hero and he is rightly regarded as an icon of one of the club's most successful periods.

> **By Petrov's third season at the club he was a true fans' favourite - the Hoops hero is rightly regarded as an icon of one of the club's most successful periods**

STILIYAN PETROV
MIDFIELDER
Celtic debut:
August 13, 1999,
League,
Dundee United 2-1 Celtic

	App	Subs	Goals
League	172	13	55
League Cup	9	5	0
Scottish Cup	15	3	5
Europe	49	2	4
Total	**245**	**23**	**64**

STILIYAN PETROV

MADE IN PARADISE | 33

STORY OF OUR LEGENDS

JIMMY DELANEY

1933 - 1946

Jimmy Delaney plied his trade with no fewer than seven clubs between 1933 and 1957 but there is no doubt that Celtic were the club of his heart, though he reached the heights throughout his entire career in Scotland, England and Ireland.

For, although he will forever be Jimmy Delaney of Celtic, his remarkable career elsewhere only added to his legend and his 'cup capers' in particular are among the most extraordinary in football.

He completed a unique hat-trick of cup-winning medals by appearing in victorious sides in the cup competitions of the SFA, the FA and Irish FA. And he came within minutes of doing a clean sweep when he reached the FAI Cup final with Cork Athletic towards the end of his career.

The cup haul started with his beloved Celtic in 1937 when Johnny Crum and Willie Buchan scored the all-important goals against Aberdeen when an astounding 146,433 fans, with thousands more locked outside, packed the old Hampden terracings.

It remains the biggest official gate for a club match in Britain but just a week earlier at the same venue Delaney played in front of 149,547 for Scotland in the 3-1 victory over England.

Delaney was a star for club and country and a firm favourite with the Celtic support. They had already enjoyed Delaney's football talents in the 1930s, and while the football during World War Two wasn't anything particularly memorable as far as Celtic were concerned, it was hoped that, post-1945, things would improve, with Delaney at the heart of a Celtic revival. Instead, the club sold the winger to Manchester United in February 1946.

Two years later he starred in the Manchester United side that defeated Blackpool 4-2 to lift the FA Cup for the first time since 1909.

By 1954 he had joined up with Derry City for an Irish record fee of £1,500 and he became the first player to win cup winners' medals in all three associations when the Brandywell club defeated Glentoran 1-0 in the final.

The following year he was on his way to Cork Athletic and in 1956 they contested the FAI Cup final with Shamrock Rovers. With just 13 minutes left on the clock, the Cork side were ahead 2-0 but the Dublin club rallied to deny the great Delaney the accolade of lifting the national cups of **FOUR** different associations.

> **Although he will forever be Jimmy Delaney of Celtic, his remarkable career elsewhere only added to his legend**

In 1946 Delaney moved south to Old Trafford for £4,000 after 13 years with Celtic. After nearly five years' service with Man United, during which time he also lifted the championship, he moved back north for a season with Aberdeen before joining Falkirk for two years ahead of his stint in Ireland with Derry and then Cork.

During his time at Celtic, as well as winning the Scottish Cup in 1937, he also won two championships in 1936 and 1938 as well as playing in the Empire Exhibition Trophy-winning side of 1938.

And Jimmy Delaney's connection to the club continued into the Millennium as his grandson, John Kennedy, also served the club as player and coach.

JIMMY DELANEY

OUTSIDE-RIGHT/ CENTRE-FORWARD

Celtic debut:
August 18, 1934, League, Hearts 0-0 Celtic

	App	Subs	Goals
League	143	n/a	69
Scottish Cup	17	n/a	5
League Cup	n/a	n/a	n/a
Europe	n/a	n/a	n/a
Total	160	n/a	74
Wartime	145	n/a	87
Total	305	n/a	161

BRIAN McCLAIR

1983 - 1987

Brian McClair was 19-years-old when he joined Celtic from Motherwell in 1983. He followed a well-worn path of strikers who moved to Celtic from Fir Park. Before him, Joe McBride and Dixie Deans joined Celtic from Motherwell. Andy Walker and Scott McDonald would later make the same journey.

Not that McClair was your conventional footballer. He had embarked on a Glasgow University course in Computer Maths and combined his studies with his early career Motherwell.

The best way for any young striker to catch the attention of bigger clubs is by scoring against them and that was McClair's forte. He grabbed a hat-trick against Rangers and a double against Celtic in two famous Motherwell wins in 1982/83. His departure to a major Scottish football power was only a matter of time after that.

Over four years, he was battling with top-class strikers for a regular place and, at one stage, was forced to play a deeper, attacking midfield role that would become his trademark at Manchester United. He delivered goals though. In each of his four seasons at Celtic, he finished top of the scoring charts for his club. His first season yielded 31 goals and he followed that up with 24 in 1984/85. He scored 26 the following season and finished up with an astonishing 41 strikes in his last campaign in the Hoops. Celtic finished that campaign empty-handed, which also happened in McClair's first season.

For someone so prolific, it must be a huge disappointment that he finished his career at Celtic with only two medals in his collection – the 1985 Scottish Cup and 1986 Scottish Premier League title. The striker was one of a select band of Celtic players who, against all odds, secured one of the most dramatic title wins in the club's history.

McClair will always cherish the role he played in Celtic winning the 1985/86 title. Hearts needed just a draw against Dundee to win the title, while Celtic were hoping for a Hearts defeat and a four-goal swing. Unbelievably, Davie Hay's side did it.

Not only did Dundee, courtesy of Albert Kidd's double, win the game 2-0, but Celtic racked up a 5-0 victory over St Mirren at Love Street to take the title on goal difference. McClair was in the thick of it. He opened the scoring with a header from Owen Archdeacon's corner and that set the tone - he was involved in two more of the goals.

By 1987, McClair was one of the best strikers in Britain. That was the same year he called time on his Celtic career, leaving to join Manchester United in the summer. The clubs were locked in a dispute over his value, which a tribunal eventually set at £850,000. Even by 1987 standards, United had got an absolute bargain.

When he was awarded a testimonial by Manchester United in 1997, there was only one team he wanted to play against, and Celtic travelled down to Old Trafford on April 15 of that year for a special tribute match in his honour.

United's side contained all the modern greats – Roy Keane, Eric Cantona and David Beckham among them. Keane scored for Man United, but Celtic, as they often did on these occasions, won the match 2-1, with Chris Hay scoring twice. A total of 44,000 supporters were there to honour McClair.

BRIAN McCLAIR

FORWARD

Celtic debut: August 24, 1983, League Cup, Brechin City 0-1 Celtic

	App	Subs	Goals
League	129	16	99
Scottish Cup	14	4	11
League Cup	19	1	9
Europe	13	3	2
Total	175	24	121

CHARLIE TULLY
1948 - 1959

Charlie Tully was born on July 11, 1924 in the Pound Loney area of Belfast, located near the Falls Road. At school, he showed an aptitude in Gaelic sports, but it didn't take long for his outstanding football ability to be recognised and he joined the books of Belfast Celtic, starting as net boy.

He made his first-team debut in 1942 and the teenager, with his bag of tricks, was soon making an impression. Loan spells at Ballyclare Comrades and Cliftonville allowed him to adjust to the physical demands of the game, and by the mid 1940s, he was a regular in the side.

Scoring the winning goal in the 1947 Irish Cup final against Glentoran further elevated 'Cheeky Charlie' in the eyes of supporters and the local Bhoy had now very much gained star-status.

Tully was actually one of a handful of men who could boast of playing for the green and white Hoops of Belfast Celtic and also of the Celtic Football Club in Glasgow. He moved to Glasgow from Belfast, having scored the winning goal in the '47 Irish Cup final, and then helping the club win the title in 1948.

Tully was in Scotland when the infamous Boxing Day match of 1948 between Belfast Celtic and Linfield took place, a game that effectively heralded the sad demise of the Irish club. Linfield fans attacked the Celtic players, with striker Jimmy Jones suffering a broken leg, and the club withdrew from the league at the end of that season, never to return.

Charlie Tully had only been a Celt for a matter of months when Rangers were the visitors to Paradise for a League Cup clash. He tormented the Ibrox side in a 3-1 win for the Hoops, leaving their famed backline 'bewildered', 'badgered' and 'mesmerised'. His dazzling display gave birth to the legend of 'Tully and Three Bears'.

Another celebrated moment in Tully's Celtic career occurred during a Scottish Cup tie away to Falkirk on February 21, 1953, when the impudent Irishman scored directly from a corner-kick. The disbelieving referee accused Tully of hitting the set-piece outside the markings and ordered a retake. Nonchalantly, Tully stepped up and repeated the feat. It was no fluke as he also managed it on international duty against England.

Tully picked up his first piece of silverware in 1951 when Celtic beat Motherwell in the Scottish Cup final. He then helped the Hoops to success in the Coronation Cup, although injury scuppered his chances of taking part in the final.

He also won the league and Scottish Cup double in 1954 and was part of the side that famously routed Rangers 7-1 in the 1957 League Cup final.

On January 31, 1959, Charlie Tully made his final start for Celtic in a home clash with Albion Rovers in the Scottish Cup first round, which the Hoops won 4-0, and on April 30, Tully announced his retirement from the game. His stay in Paradise was at an end after 11 years. He had made 319 appearances for the club and scored 43 goals.

Tragically, Charlie Tully died suddenly back home in Belfast on July 27, 1971 at the age of just 47.

> **Tully tormented the Ibrox side in a 3-1 win for the Hoops, leaving their famed backline 'bewildered', 'badgered' and 'mesmerised'. His dazzling display gave birth to the legend of 'Tully and Three Bears'**

CHARLIE TULLY
INSIDE-LEFT
Celtic debut:
November 27, 1971, League,
Partick Thistle 1-5 Celtic
(scored once)

	App	Subs	Goals
League	216	n/a	30
Scottish Cup	35	n/a	6
League Cup	68	n/a	7
Europe	n/a	n/a	n/a
Total	**319**	**n/a**	**43**

JACKIE McNAMARA
1995 - 2005

Jackie McNamara followed in his father's footsteps when he joined Celtic in 1995, with Jackie senior having spent six years with the Hoops between 1970-76.

But while the latter would only make 43 appearances for the club before moving to Hibernian to establish his reputation there, the former played 359 times for Celtic, including 307 starts. He spent 10 years with the club, was involved in some of the major triumphs of the time, and was also rewarded with a testimonial for his service to the club.

McNamara was fiercely competitive throughout his time at Celtic, adding to the obvious ability he possessed, and he was a right-back of style and substance for the Hoops.

He was part of the squad which 'stopped the 10' in 1998 and then played his part in the many successes the club enjoyed under Martin O'Neill. McNamara was a quiet personality, but also a determined one, and never let the team down.

He had joined Dunfermline Athletic's youth set-up as a 17-year-old in September 1991, and he made his first-team debut the following year in a 3-0 defeat to Arbroath. On Bert Paton's appointment in 1993, he became the regular right-back at East End Park and was soon causing a stir with his performances.

Adventurous, skilful and comfortable in possession, McNamara emerged as a potent attacking weapon for the Pars as they narrowly missed out on promotion from the First Division. The Fifers endured a similar scenario the following season as Aberdeen defeated them in a play-off, but McNamara, who had already been capped eight times for Scotland Under-21s, was always going to be destined for career at the top and his departure was close at hand.

The new Bhoy was soon into full stride in his new surroundings. His enterprising runs from the right-back, skill on the ball and crossing ability made him a firm favourite among supporters. However, McNamara was such a talented footballer that he was capable of playing in any number of positions, and he would enjoy one of his greatest seasons when deployed in a more advanced role by Wim Jansen.

Under the Dutchman, Celtic managed to win their first league title in 10 years, stopping Rangers from reaching 10-in-a-row, and lift the League Cup. McNamara was recognised for his pivotal role in this success by being awarded the Player of the Year accolade from his peers.

During Martin O'Neill's reign, McNamara wasn't initially an automatic starter, not helped by a change in system, but remained a vital squad player. He could always be relied upon when needed as was the case in the 2001 Scottish Cup final. Having entered the fray as a substitute for the injured Lubo Moravcik, he scored the opening goal in a 3-0 victory over Hibernian to seal the club's first treble in over 30 years.

McNamara's versatility saw him rise to prominence once again in the 2003/04 season. He maintained the same high standards in a variety of positions to help Celtic achieve the double and the Scottish writers named him as their Player of the Year.

His growing influence was underlined when O'Neill awarded him the captaincy in the following season. And the day after leading the Hoops to another Scottish Cup triumph in what was his last game, Celtic took on Ireland in his testimonial as reward for his decade of service, a memorable moment for the boyhood Hoops fan.

JACKIE McNAMARA

RIGHT-BACK
Celtic debut: October 4, 1995, League, Falkirk 0-1 Celtic

	App	Subs	Goals
League	221	36	10
Scottish Cup	25	5	3
League Cup	17	2	1
Europe	43	9	1
Total	**307**	**52**	**15**

PATSY GALLACHER

1911 – 1926

Anyone looking at Patsy Gallacher, standing tall at five feet, seven inches, and weighing in at nine stone, ten pounds, would have dismissed his chances of making it in the tough, physical world of association football.

Indeed, some might have worried that he would survive just one appearance on a pitch. Yet, he would play 464 times for Celtic, scoring 192 goals, and his career, which began with the Hoops in November 1911 when he was just 18-years-old, would go on until he retired as a Falkirk player in 1932. He had just turned 39 two weeks prior to that.

The official height given for Patsy Gallacher on his debut against St Mirren in December 1911, is 5'5" although some sources list him as being 5'6", 5'7" and 5'9"! Weighing around seven stones, there was a real fear that the 18-year-old would be seriously hurt amid the hurly-burly of Scotland's top flight. 'Boys, meet your new inside-right,' said Willie Maley when he introduced the new signing from Clydebank. 'Willie,' responded an incredulous Jimmy Quinn, 'if you put that wee thing out on the park you'll get done for manslaughter!' The concerns

proved to be unfounded as 'Charlie Chaplin's double' was 'tricky', 'elusive' and showed 'cool artfulness', becoming 'a favourite in his first match'. In that 3-1 win over St Mirren, a Celtic legend was born.

The Bhoy from Donegal was the creative genius that Willie Maley injected into the team and who inspired Celtic to four league titles in a row between 1914-17. He was also at the core of all of Celtic's subsequent triumphs up to the 1925 Scottish Cup triumph, which is known to this day as 'The Patsy Gallacher Final'.

Patsy lost his balance no fewer than three times and recovered, with the ball still at his feet, when he scored his most memorable strike in the Scottish Cup final on April 11, 1925. Celtic were a goal behind to Dundee with 20 minutes to go when Patsy took possession and an eyewitness, newspaper account captures the moment perfectly. 'He jinked, jouked, hurdled, swerved, dribbled, jumped, fell, got up, ran on, jinked again, stumbled, jouked once more, went over his wilkies with the ball still grasped between his feet and suddenly, he was over the line, him and the ball, past an astonished Jock Britton, and Hampden to the last 75,000th man was rising in starry-eyed tribute to a genius in bootlaces.' Minutes later he almost went through again, with Jimmy McGrory going on to score a late winner.

His first and last medals for the club came in the Scottish Cup and he scored in both finals, in 1912 and 1925. The latter, which kick-started Celtic's comeback in a 2-1 win over Dundee, will go down in history as one of the best cup final goals of all time, anywhere in the world.

Over the course of his 15-year Celtic career, he added another two Scottish Cup triumphs – in 1914 and 1923 – to bring his overall tally to four. Gallacher also won a total of six championships with Celtic. He was an integral part of the four-in-a-row run between 1914 and 1917, and was a virtual ever-present in seasons 1918/19 and 1921/22 as Celtic were again crowned champions of Scotland. The 1921/22 triumph, coming 10 years after he had signed for Celtic, must have been especially sweet for Gallacher. It also turned out to be the last league title he won during his Celtic career. Celtic would win the title in 1926, but Gallacher played a solitary game that season, ruled out for the campaign through injury.

PATSY GALLACHER

INSIDE-RIGHT
Celtic debut: December 2, 1911, League, Celtic 3-1 St Mirren

	App	Subs	Goals
League	432	n/a	186
Scottish Cup	32	n/a	6
League Cup	n/a	n/a	n/a
Europe	n/a	n/a	n/a
Total	464	n/a	192

PATSY GALLACHER

The Bhoy from Donegal was the creative genius that Willie Maley injected into the team and who inspired Celtic to four league titles in a row between 1914-17

STORY OF OUR LEGENDS

DAVIE HAY

1965 - 1974

When Celtic reached their centenary season in 1987/88, only six men had ever managed the club during that first 100 years and all of them had worn the green and white as a player.

Among that half-dozen was Davie Hay and, as a dyed-in-the-wool Celtic supporter all his days, it is something he is immensely proud of.

He has also served the club in other backroom roles over the years and his love for the club in that time has never diminished.

He joined the club as a schoolboy in the mid 1960s just as the Hoops were beginning to make inroads on the continent and, by the end of the decade, he was a fixture in the first team and also became one of only 16 Celtic players to have played in a European Cup final.

He had made his debut two years before that 1970 final against Feyenoord in Milan's San Siro when, in a league game, he came on as a sub in a 4-1 victory over Aberdeen at Celtic Park and that was the first of nearly 200 games before moving to Chelsea in 1974.

He was at the peak of his career then and seemingly a stick-on for every Scotland international but injury curtailed his career and he turned to coaching and management at an early age.

During his time with the club he lifted five championships, two Scottish Cups and a League Cup as well as playing in that European Cup final, a hefty haul for a 26-year-old.

On having to give up the playing side of the game, he took up coaching at Chelsea and moved to Motherwell where he eventually became manager before returning to take up that post at Celtic at the age only 35-years-old.

He led the team to the Scottish Cup victory of season 1984/85 in the 100th final when the Hoops beat Dundee United 2-1 thanks to goals from Davie Provan and Frank McGarvey.

However, despite that milestone capture of world football's oldest trophy, it was winning the league title the following season against all odds that was to carve a new chapter in Celtic's history.

Despite trailing Hearts and spending much of the latter half of the season flitting between third, fourth and fifth place, Davie Hay's Celts went on an unbeaten run of 13 games, winning the last eight of those games, losing only two goals in the process, with no fewer than six of those games played in the month of April, leaving the final game at Love Street on May 3.

Hearts were playing Dundee at Dens Park and only need a draw while, if they lost by one goal, Celtic would have to win by three clear goals.

It looked impossible but, in his home town of Paisley, Davie Hay's side sped to a 5-0 win while, amazingly, Dundee sub, Albert Kidd came on and scored the only two goals of the game at Dens Park – one of Celtic's most amazing title wins was done and dusted in the most incredible fashion.

He returned to Celtic as chief scout in 1994, became assistant general manager in 1997 when he was instrumental behind the scenes in bringing Henrik Larsson to Celtic Park and was later made Club Ambassador.

Davie Hay is an all-time Hoops legend and one of only 15 Celts to be name-checked in the lyrics of The Willie Maley Song.

DAVIE HAY

MIDFIELDER
Celtic debut:
March 6, 1968 (substitute),
League,
Celtic 4-1 Aberdeen

	App	Subs	Goals
League	106	3	6
Scottish Cup	24	0	1
League Cup	37	0	5
Europe	23	0	0
Total	**190**	**3**	**12**

PAUL LAMBERT

1997 - 2005

Listing the achievements and trajectory of Paul Lambert's career from its humble beginning to its title-laden climax reads like something out of *Roy of the Rovers*.

Within 10 years the former Celtic captain had gone from lifting the Scottish Cup with St Mirren, the last team comprised of all Scots to do so, to helping Borussia Dortmund lift the European Cup in the first season of its new incarnation as the UEFA Champions League.

Lauded for his man-marking job of Juventus' playmaker Zinedine Zidane in the final, Lambert was also the provider for the first of Karl-Heinz Riedle's double that night in Munich, making him the first Scot to win the cup with a non-UK team.

Lambert started his career in Paisley in the mid-1980s, spending nine years with the Buddies before moving to Motherwell where he helped the Steelmen to two top-three finishes in the league in consecutive years.

He was first spotted by Dortmund manager Ottmar Hitzfeld while playing for the Lanarkshire side against the Bundesliga outfit and it wasn't long before he joined the German giants, moving there in 1996.

It only took a year on the continent before Scotland came calling, however, in the shape of Celtic, who were in desperate need of a midfield general to help them stop Rangers' stranglehold on the league title.

The Celts' famous nine-in-a-row record had been matched in the 1996/97 season and Lambert was one of a number of players signed by Wim Jansen to help stop the dreaded 10.

Success came early for Lambert at Celtic as he helped the Bhoys lift the League Cup in his maiden season, but his first true telling impact came in the New Year derby 2-0 win over Rangers when his thumping 30-yard effort sealed the game for the Celts to mark a turning point in the title race.

He went on to hold down a regular place in that historic season and helped the Hoops to their first league title in 10 years to preserve the record set by Jock Stein's side from the 1960s and '70s.

Lambert's combative yet classy approach to the game soon saw him become the linchpin of the Celtic midfield, anchored by Neil Lennon at his side and Stiliyan Petrov ahead of him and he was promoted to captain under Martin O'Neill following the magnificent treble-winning season of 2000/01.

He helped carry the Bhoys to the UEFA Cup final in 2003 and enjoyed the golden era of his playing career under O'Neill, giving Celtic fans a truly world-class, home-grown midfielder to support, the likes of which hadn't been seen since Paul McStay.

In his seven years at the club, Lambert amassed four league titles, two Scottish Cups, two League Cups and a Scottish Football Writers' Association Player of the Year award, underlining his own personal quality but also the elite level of player he starred alongside at the turn of the century.

Lambert's performances at club level were also recognised by the national team and he collected a total of 40 caps for Scotland in a career that saw him play in World Cup 1998 and captain his country.

His playing career came to a close when he took a player/manager role at Livingston, his first foray into coaching, and he has since gone on to hold positions at Wycombe, Colchester, Norwich, Aston Villa and Blackburn, but Lambert will always be remembered for his success at Celtic and is rightly regarded as a Hoops legend.

PAUL LAMBERT

MIDFIELDER
Celtic debut:
August 11, 1997,
League,
Rangers 1-0 Celtic

	App	Subs	Goals
League	180	12	14
Scottish Cup	19	4	1
League Cup	10	1	2
Europe	44	3	2
Total	**253**	**20**	**19**

STORY OF OUR LEGENDS

ALEC McNAIR
1904 - 1925

Alec McNair made his Celtic debut in January 1905 at the age of 21. He played his last game for the Hoops in April 1925 at the age of 41 years and 113 days, making him the oldest player to represent Celtic.

That, in itself, is a remarkable achievement, and in an era when there was no European football and the League Cup was still four decades away from being set up, his appearance tally of 641 is testament to his value to Celtic over many seasons.

He also played for 10 years of his Celtic career having to cope with personal tragedy. His wife had died in August 1915, leaving him to bring up their five children on his own. This he did while also working a 12-hour shift in wartime work, forging metal for horseshoes at the Munitions Industry factory in his home town of Bo'ness. He did all that while still trying to keep fit and playing for Celtic every Saturday.

His contribution was vital in delivering success to the club, most notably the six-in-a-row triumph of 1905-10 and the subsequent four-in-a-row between 1914-17.

During that time, Celtic won the double in consecutive seasons, in 1907 and 1908, and were only denied the chance of a third successive double success when the Scottish Cup was withheld following crowd trouble at the end of the replay of the final against Rangers, which had finished 1-1.

Alec McNair's medal haul was staggering. Having won six titles in the first decade of the 20th century, he was also part of the next great Celtic team that Maley created, winning those four titles between 1914-17 and only denied a repeat of their six-in-a-row success due to Rangers winning a solitary championship in 1918 before Celtic regained the title.

Over and above that, there was also the six Scottish Cup triumphs, while his total medal haul stands at 36, if you include the eight Glasgow Cups and 10 Charity Cups that he won.

There were also some remarkable feats during this time. In the 1908/09 league win, Celtic played their last eight games in just 11 days, winning five of them, drawing two and losing just one. Alec McNair played in all of those matches.

And in season 1915/16, Celtic played and won two league matches on the same day. They beat Raith Rovers 6-0 at Celtic Park, with Patsy Gallacher the hat-trick hero that day, and then headed straight for Fir Park to face Motherwell. They ran out 3-1 winners in that second game. Not surprisingly, Alec McNair was in the team for both of those games.

It was on April 18, 1925 that Alec McNair took to the field for the last time in the green and white Hoops as Celtic drew 1-1 with Queen's Park at Celtic Park, Paddy Connolly scoring the goal in the second-last game of the campaign. In doing so McNair, was, and still, is the oldest player to represent Celtic.

> **McNair also played for 10 years of his Celtic career having to cope with personal tragedy. His wife had died in August 1915, leaving him to bring up their five children on his own. This he did while also working a 12-hour shift forging metal**

He was 41 years and 113 days old when the game took place with him at right-back, while Hugh Hilley took up the left-back berth. Hilly was just five-years-old when McNair made his Celtic debut 21 years earlier in 1905.

ALEC McNAIR

UTILITY/RIGHT-BACK
Celtic debut:
January 3, 1905,
League,
Celtic 2-3 Airdrie

	App	Subs	Goals
League	584	n/a	9
Scottish Cup	57	n/a	0
League Cup	n/a	n/a	n/a
Europe	n/a	n/a	n/a
Total	**641**	**n/a**	**9**

FAMOUS FIVE

No.2 - Oh, Hampden in the Sun

On the Sunday morning of October 20, 1957, both sides of the Glasgow divide awoke with a hangover to beat them all.

The blue half of the city suffered the self-induced torment of sorrows far too colossal to be drowned by mere alcohol while those of a green persuasion cursed the Draconian licensing laws that curtailed, temporarily at least, their thirst to celebrate 90 minutes of unforgettable football from the previous day.

The Celtic history books don't necessarily record what the weather was like on that late Autumn Sabbath but we do know that conditions 24 hours earlier were very clement indeed - and not just meteorologically.

The very refrain of *Oh, Hampden in the Sun*, a pastiche of Harry Belafonte's contemporaneous chart hit *Island In The Sun* - a parody which is still sung to this day, continually reminds us of the glorious sunshine that beamed down upon Glasgow that day.

It was the biggest winning margin ever recorded in a top-grade British cup final and the heroes from the October Revolution of 1957 have been acclaimed in book and in song but can those of us who were not around in 1957 fully appreciate what was achieved by the Hoops that day?

Sammy Wilson opened the scoring in the 23rd minute but amazingly Celtic could have been four up by that time and hit the woodwork three times in the first half before Neilly Mochan scored the second just before the break.

The half-time score of 2-0 warned no-one of what was to come and eight minutes after the break Billy McPhail hit the first of his hat-trick before Simpson pulled one back for the Ibrox side.

There was no stopping the Celtic torrent on the Rangers goal, though. McPhail got his second, Mochan did likewise five minutes later and McPhail completed his trio before Willie Fernie finished the rout with a penalty in the last minute.

Those who witnessed the demolition paid 2/- (10p) for entry to the terracing and 9d (4p) for the Boys' Gate but it's doubtful if a 13-year-old Jimmy Johnstone paid in.

His father took him to his first big game that day from Uddingston on a Celtic supporters' bus and it's a pound to a penny he got a lift-over (even as a Lisbon Lion 10 years later he would probably have got a lift-over).

And what was future Lisbon Lion captain Billy McNeill doing that day? Amazingly, there was still a full professional card on that day and the minor leagues were no different. The 17-year-old McNeill was on duty having been farmed out to Blantyre Vics and he didn't know the score until he bought an evening paper at Motherwell bus station!

So although, like McNeill, the vast majority of the crowd who turn up at Paradise every other week will not have seen the 7-1 game (especially since it mysteriously disappeared from the TV screens that night) we still have the opportunity to hail them in song.

PAUL McSTAY

1981 - 1997

If ever a nickname summed up a player to perfection, then it is The Maestro ... because that's exactly what Paul McStay was. For 16 years he was the model of perfection in the middle of the park for Celtic, an exceptionally talented player who was also the personification of 'faithful through and through'. He enjoyed good times with the club, particularly in the 1980s, but also endured a tougher period in the early '90s.

For 16 years The Maestro was the model of perfection in the middle of the park for Celtic, an exceptionally talented player who was also the personification of 'faithful through and through'

Throughout it all, Paul McStay performed to the highest level. If his shoulders stoop at all today, it is because he carried the team and the hopes of the support for six years, between their Scottish Cup triumph of 1989 and the victory over Airdrie six years later in the same competition.

The McStay name is one of the most famous in Celtic's history, with Paul's great-uncles, Willie and Jimmy, club legends of the pre-Second World War era. Paul's brother, Willie, also played for the club in the '80s, and the two brothers enjoyed a number of successes, including both scoring in a victory over Rangers. Yet, the best of them all was Paul Michael Lyons McStay.

He announced his presence to the football world, not in the green and white of Celtic, and not at his beloved Paradise. Instead it was in the dark blue of Scotland, in a schoolboy international match against England at Wembley. The 1980 match saw Scotland win 5-4, with McStay scoring twice and inspiring the Scots to a memorable victory.

A week after his Celtic debut, he scored the first of his 72 goals for the club in an impressive 3-1 victory for the Hoops at Pittodrie, receiving the ball on the edge of the 18-yard box before wiggling past two Aberdeen defenders and lashing the ball in with

PAUL McSTAY

MIDFIELDER
Celtic debut: January 23, 1982, Scottish Cup,
Celtic 4-0 Queen of the South

	App	Subs	Goals
League	509	6	57
Scottish Cup	66	0	6
League Cup	54	0	7
Europe	42	0	2
Total	**671**	**6**	**72**

PAUL McSTAY

his left foot. This was to be the one of the first signs that Celtic had a special talent on their hands.

Paul McStay won seven major trophies during his time at Celtic. His talent deserved much more. He played 10 games in the championship-winning season of 1981/82 after breaking into the team in January 1982, and the following season he won his first trophy as part of the Celtic team which enjoyed a rare League Cup triumph. His two league title successes, however, rank alongside the most memorable in Celtic's history.

In 1986, Davie Hay's side had managed to put together a run of victories that exerted pressure on league leaders, Hearts. However, going into the last game of the season, Celtic needed to win by at least three clear goals at Love Street and hope that Hearts lost at Dens Park. In the event, the Bhoys, wearing their lime-green away shirts and inspired by Paul McStay, ran out 5-0 winners, with the Maestro scoring one of the goals. Dundee beat Hearts 2-0 and so the title returned to Paradise.

Two years later, Celtic celebrated their centenary season, with Billy McNeill back at the helm. A league and cup double duly followed, with the Maestro conducting the team in the centre of the park. It was Paul McStay's finest season as a Celt, which is a bold statement, given his quality and consistency year in, year out. There would be two further triumphs – a Scottish Cup triumph over Rangers in 1989, and then another Scottish Cup win in 1995, which allowed Paul McStay to lift a trophy as a Celtic captain.

STORY OF OUR LEGENDS

NEIL LENNON
2000 - 2007

Neil Lennon joined a team packed with quality players, and took his place comfortably alongside them. He also became an instant favourite with the fans. He was one of them and they took him to their hearts.

He also had to contend with a level of hatred and hostility away from the pitch that has rarely, if ever been experienced by anyone else, certainly not by any other sports person. He handled it all with dignity and courage.

The club were dominant domestically and set about re-establishing their reputation on the European stage, which culminated in the 2003 UEFA Cup final.

And when he took over as manager at Celtic Park, Neil Lennon continued to deliver success, including three league titles in a row and consecutive appearances in the last 16 of the Champions League, as well as the memorable victory over Barcelona on a night that Paradise will never forget.

When Martin O'Neill was appointed manager in 2000, speculation was rife that Neil Lennon would follow him from Leicester City. It took around six months, but eventually, O'Neill got his man.

He enjoyed a stellar playing career in Paradise, amassing an incredible amount of silverware as Celtic held sway in Scottish football. In his first season, he

helped the club to their first domestic treble in over 30 years. By the time he left Paradise in 2007, he had won five league championships, four Scottish Cups and two League Cups. He also was a member of the side that memorably reached the 2003 UEFA Cup final in Seville, and played his part in some wonderful UEFA Champions League victories over the likes of Manchester United, Juventus, Lyon and Porto. Along with this all this success, the Irishman was bestowed the club captaincy when Gordon Strachan took the helm in 2005, becoming the first of his countrymen to officially skipper Celtic since Bertie Peacock back in the 1950s.

It was fitting that Lennon should end his Celtic playing career on a high note as he captained the club to success in the 2007 Scottish Cup final.

The low points of Neil Lennon's time

46 | MADE IN PARADISE

NEIL LENNON

at the club, of course, came off the field, where he attracted an unprecedented and unacceptable level of hostility which had its roots, sadly, in anti-Irish attitudes that still exist amongst some people in Scotland. Given that the hostility included death threats and bombs being sent through the post to him, as well as assaults in city streets, his attitude is a credit to him.

It wasn't long before Neil Lennon was back at Celtic Park as a coach under Gordon Strachan. When Tony Mowbray left in March 2010, Lennon was appointed interim manager and was awarded the job permanently. His full tally as manager was three championships and two Scottish Cups and when Celtic secured the league and Scottish Cup in 2012/13, he wrote himself into the history books by following Jock Stein and Billy McNeill in winning the double both a Celtic player and a manager.

Neil Lennon will always be remembered as a winning Celtic player and winning Celtic manager. It's what he always hoped for.

NEIL LENNON
MIDFIELDER
Celtic debut:
December 10, 2000,
League,
Dundee 1-2 Celtic

	App	Subs	Goals
League	212	2	3
Scottish Cup	26	0	0
League Cup	10	1	0
Europe	52	1	0
Total	**300**	**4**	**3**

The Irishman was bestowed the club captaincy when Gordon Strachan took the helm in 2005, becoming the first of his countrymen to officially skipper Celtic since Bertie Peacock

STORY OF OUR LEGENDS

WILLIE FERNIE

1948 - 1958, 1960 - 1961

Willie Fernie had trials with both Aberdeen and Raith Rovers and in his late teens he could have had the pick of clubs on moving on from Leslie Hearts, but it was Celtic scout Pat Duffy who secured the services of this silky player who was a natural-born dribbler.

He signed for Celtic on October 12, 1948, and was then farmed out to Fife side, Kinglassie Colliery. It would be a year-and-a-half before he made the first of his Celtic debuts and he had a decent medal haul in the 1950s with the Coronation Cup, when he replaced the injured Charlie Tully in the final against Hibernian, the league and Scottish Cup double of 1953/54 and two League Cup final wins in 1956/57 and 1957/58.

In the 1957 League Cup final 7-1 win over Rangers, it was in final minute of a match that Fernie created a much-celebrated piece of Celtic history with his penalty strike at 'Hampden in the Sun'.

By the 90th minute of the 1957 League Cup final, he and his Celtic team-mates had thumped in six and had hit the post a further four times in what was a complete rout of their derby rivals.

Rangers were on the rack, a broken and spent force with full-back, John Valentine and goalkeeper, George Niven enduring a nightmare afternoon. Then, with seconds remaining, the outstanding Billy McPhail was unceremoniously flattened inside the box.

Fernie was the man who stepped up to take the resulting spot-kick, aiming for Niven's bunnet in the back corner of the goal. The penalty was duly tucked away and one of the club's finest 90 minutes sealed in the perfect fashion.

He left for Middlesbrough on December 1, 1958, but returned on October 6, 1960 and two days later he made his second debut for the Hoops.

Before departing for St Mirren in November, 1961 his last act on the pitch as a Celt was to score the second goal in a 2-2 draw with Rangers at Ibrox on September 16.

Willie Fernie was an outstanding football talent and one of Celtic's finest players of the 1950s. He was also, in later years, an important part of the backroom staff at the club, helping to nurture the group of exceptionally talented players coming through at that time who were known as the Quality Street Gang. He was also described by Brian Clough as one of the finest providers he ever played alongside, during their stint together at Middlesbrough.

He could also boast of having played in two World Cups for Scotland, in Switzerland (1954) and Sweden (1958), and was capped a total of 12 times for his country.

But his major contribution was to Celtic, and he was always an elegant presence in the starting XI for the green and white Hoops.

On leaving Celtic for the second time, he joined St Mirren and spent over 18 months at Love Street before trialling with Partick Thistle and having short spells with Alloa, Fraserburgh, Coleraine under former team-mate Bertie Peacock and Bangor under Charlie Tully before retiring in 1965

He then returned to Celtic as reserve coach in June 1967 and he ran the rule over an emerging bunch of youngsters over the next few years as players such as Kenny Dalglish, Danny McGrain, Lou Macari, Davie Hay, George Connelly and many others had the undoubted benefit of the experience of a true Celtic great.

> **Willie had a decent medal haul in the 1950s with the Coronation Cup, a league and Scottish Cup double and two League Cups**

WILLIE FERNIE
INSIDE-FORWARD
Celtic debut:
March 18, 1950,
League,
St Mirren 0-1 Celtic

	App	Subs	Goals
League	219	n/a	54
Scottish Cup	39	n/a	10
League Cup	59	n/a	11
Europe	n/a	n/a	n/a
Total	317	n/a	75

FAMOUS FIVE

No.3 - Champions of Europe

On September 28, 1966, a twin strikeforce of Stevie Chalmers and Joe McBride kicked off Celtic's first ever game in the European Cup…

And little did those watching in the 50,000 crowd realise that just eight months and nine games later, an 85th-minute reflex strike from Chalmers would see the trophy paraded at the very ground where they were standing in the East End of Glasgow.

McBride was to get on the scoreline that night but not before Tommy Gemmell had scored the club's first ever European Cup goal in the 2-0 win over Swiss champions FC Zurich and Celtic's European dream began in earnest.

That was followed with a 3-0 away win and those few wide-eyed optimists who had started saving for a European Cup final as soon as the Celts clinched their first championship in 12 years breathed a contented sigh.

France was next and when Nantes took a 16th-minute lead in the first leg, things didn't look quite so rosy but the Celts equalised before half-time and two further goals gave the Bhoys an impressive 3-1 away win.

By the 13th minute of the home leg, the 41,000 crowd were already looking forward to the quarter-final draw as Jimmy Johnstone had fired Celtic 4-1 ahead on aggregate.

The French champions levelled before the break but crosses from Johnstone unlocked the Nantes defence to provide goals for Chalmers and Bobby Lennox for a commanding 6-2 aggregate score.

If the fans didn't know much about Zurich or Nantes before their heroes played them, then Vojvodina would be a real step into the dark for supporters and players alike.

The Yugoslavian side welcomed the Celts for the first leg and weren't the most generous of hosts when they took, and held, a 1-0 lead.

The Celts had it all to do a week later but with no fewer than 75,000 urging them on, there had to be a chance that they could do it.

However, despite Chalmers giving them the lead as the game approached the hour mark, the preceding 30 minutes heralded no further goals and thoughts turned towards a play-off scheduled for Rotterdam if the stalemate prevailed.

There was one last throw of the dice though when Johnstone won a corner on the right in the 90th minute and Charlie Gallagher placed the ball to take the kick.

The same player delivered the corner that won the Scottish Cup two years earlier against Dunfermline to kick-off Celtic's silver-laden run when the forehead of Billy McNeill met the ball and channelled it into the net…

And history was repeated here to possibly even greater effect as the skipper powered a header into the back of the net just seconds before the ref blew the final whistle.

Dukla Prague awaited in the semi-final and another 75,000 crowd spurred the Celts on in the first leg at Paradise as a 1-1 half-time scoreline was improved upon by the Celts in the second 45 when Willie Wallace got in on the European goalscoring act with two goals after the turnaround.

The 3-1 first-leg advantage taken over to Prague wasn't going to be given up lightly.

In the European Cup-Winners' Cup semi-final of season 1963/64, the Celts travelled to MTK Budapest 'protecting' a 3-0 lead but contrived to lose 4-0 over there.

In Jock Stein's eyes, the risk was too great and Celtic adopted damage limitations policy which had previously been alien to the club and its supporters – but it worked, the Celts drew 0-0, won 3-1 on aggregate and were in the European Cup final at the first time of asking.

Lisbon and Inter Milan awaited and the greatest day in the history of Celtic football club was to unfold…

Celtic 2 Inter Milan 1 tells its own story but there are a million-and-one stories arising from that May evening and the days that followed.

And they still sound as fresh and exciting as we can still hear the mighty Lions roar.

STORY OF OUR LEGENDS

LISBON LIONS
Stand

RONNIE SIMPSON

1964 - 1970

Ronnie Simpson made his senior football debut for Queen's Park at the age of 14. It would be fully two decades before he took his Celtic bow – but that didn't stop him going on to become an all-time Hoops great.

In what was only Celtic's third European campaign, Ronnie first appeared for the club on October 18, 1964 - as the Hoops lost 3-1 to Barcelona in the first leg of an Inter Cities Fairs Cup tie in Spain.

The experienced Simpson, signed for £4,000 by Sean Fallon, made a total of 10 appearances for the club that season, but in 1965/66 – Jock Stein's first full season in charge – he established himself as Celtic's No.1, making a total of 48 starts as the Hoops won the first of nine consecutive Scottish titles.

Having started his career at Hampden before going on to play with Third Lanark and Hibernian, Ronnie had played at Celtic Park several times during the early years of his career.

Indeed, the record books showed that he kept goal for Queen's Park against the Hoops at Celtic Park on Christmas Day, 1946. Many of his future Lisbon Lions team-mates would have still been in their nappies at that point.

RONNIE SIMPSON

GOALKEEPER
Celtic debut:
November 18, 1964,
Fairs Cities' Cup,
Barcelona 3-1 Celtic

	App	Subs	Goals
League	118	0	0
Scottish Cup	17	0	0
League Cup	29	0	0
Europe	24	0	0
Total	**188**	**0**	**0**

RONNIE SIMPSON

Nicknamed 'Faither' by the Lisbon Lions squad, he was held in the utmost respect by everyone at Celtic during his time at the club

He had a spell at Newcastle United, where he won FA Cup medals in 1952 and 1955, and although he didn't play in their 1951 win, it did see him head north to play in a cup winners' match against the Scottish Cup holders at Celtic Park on September 12, 1951 – the game finished 3-3.

During his Celtic career, he won four league championships, one Scottish Cup, two League Cups and, of course, the European Cup.

Season 1966/67 marked the high point in Simpson's career. He was named Scotland's Player of the Year as Celtic won every tournament they entered and became the first British side to win the European Cup.

Simpson, at the age of 36, was one of the stars of Celtic's most successful side. Stein, who had managed Simpson at Hibs and actually sold him to Celtic, kept faith with the elder statesman of his side and was rewarded with a string of fine performances from Glasgow-born No.1.

Nicknamed 'Faither' by the Lisbon Lions squad, he was held in the utmost respect by everyone at Celtic during his time at the club and is still classed as one of the best goalkeepers to have played for the Bhoys.

He also won five Scotland caps – his first coming at the age of 36 years and

196 days. Typically, it was the day Scotland beat the World Champions, England, 3-2 at Wembley. He had also represented Great Britain at 1948 Olympics in England.

In terms of shut-outs, Simpson's record – 91 in 188 games - stands comparison to that of any goalkeeper in Celtic's history.

His final game on October 13, 1969, in the League Cup semi-final against Ayr United, took him to that tally – which mirrors that of another legendary Celtic goalkeeper, John Thomson.

Simpson had to be replaced by Willie Wallace after dislocating his shoulder – with Tommy Gemmell taking over in goals.

It was the last time the Celtic fans would see him in action, although he stayed at the club until May 1970 – when he officially retired at the age of 39.

After leaving Celtic, he managed Hamilton Accies for a short time.

DANNY McGRAIN

1967 - 1987

Danny McGrain started in schools' football with Camus Place Primary and Kingsridge Secondary and caught the eye of the club while playing for Scottish Schools at Ibrox.

Legend has it that Rangers approached the young player but on hearing that his name was Daniel Fergus McGrain, they wrongly presumed he was Catholic and didn't pursue the matter further. The same day he played at Ibrox, May 13, 1967, Sean Fallon was sitting with the youngster's parents when he got home and he signed for Celtic that day.

He was farmed out to both Queen's Park Victoria XI and Maryhill Juniors while another recent signing, Kenny Dalglish did likewise with Cumbernauld United. It soon became apparent that this group of Celtic reserves, who would soon pick up the epithet, the Quality Street Gang, would be worthy challengers to the Lisbon Lions in the first team.

Three days after his debut, the fifth consecutive league flag was raised at Celtic Park. At the age of 39, Bobby Collins played in that game in the blue and white hoops of Morton – Danny McGrain wasn't even born when Bobby played his first game for Celtic.

There were a multitude of highs for Danny McGrain in a career in which he started off mixing with the Lisbon Lions and carried on through to the late 1980s – just missing out on the glory of the centenary year.

There were six league championships, five Scottish Cups and two League Cups for the player who was considered the finest right-back in the world. His first two championships were part of the nine-in-a-row sequence and his final three were as skipper as he was the proud captain of the Hoops for a decade.

Not only was he around at the time of Lisbon and around for most of the nine-in-a-row years, he also skippered the club in two

> **There were six league championships, five Scottish Cups and two League Cups for the player who was considered the finest right-back in the world**

of their most famous title-clinchers – the 4-2 game of 1979 and the last-gasp glory of Love Street in 1986.

Indeed, his first and last appearances for Celtic both featured on the front page of the *Celtic View*. The first after making the breakthrough as a 20-year-old and the last after playing his part in the magnificent 5-0 win over St Mirren in Paisley when Dundee's 2-0 defeat of Hearts at Dens Park also helped win the title in the most dramatic of circumstances.

His first league appearance heralded the raising of a flag and his last on May 3, 1986 delivered one.

Danny McGrain overcame various obstacles in his career, including a fractured skull in 1972, he was diagnosed with diabetes in 1974 and an ankle injury in 1977 also threatened to finish his career.

He tackled the diabetes a vigorously as he tackled some of the world's best players and it is to his credit that he didn't let it affect his career and he became a role model for future players who were diabetics.

However, if it weren't for injuries, he may well have been challenging Billy McNeill at the top of the Celtic appearance charts.

DANNY McGRAIN

RIGHT-BACK
Celtic debut:
August 26, 1970 (substitute),
League Cup,
Dundee United 2-2 Celtic

	App	Subs	Goals
League	433	8	4
Scottish Cup	60	0	1
League Cup	105	1	3
Europe	55	1	0
Total	**653**	**10**	**8**

DANNY McGRAIN

STORY OF OUR LEGENDS

WILLIE WALLACE
1966 - 1971

There can't be many transfers in football which were as successful as Willie Wallace's move from Hearts to Celtic towards the end of 1966.

Within six short months, 'Wispy' and his goals had helped fire Jock Stein's all-conquering side to the league championship, the Scottish Cup and, most memorably, the European Cup in Lisbon. It was the most glorious season in the club's history.

For the next five years, the striker maintained his prolific form in front of goal and collected numerous winner's medals as the Hoops continued their dominance of domestic football and reached another European Cup final.

Prior to that, though, the striker certainly showed a bit of adventure when he signed for Celtic as he was looking for a move to Canada at the time and Stoke City and Newcastle United were also checking out the player who, unbelievably had been playing at Tynecastle without a contract for two years.

Both sides were offering around £80,000 for the striker but he moved to Celtic Park for £28,000.

Despite Hearts coming within a hairsbreadth of winning the title in 1964/65, the League Cup in season 1962/63 was his only winner's medal before joining the Hoops. However, within months of signing on the dotted line with Celtic, he had a full set of domestic medals and a European Cup one to boot.

There can be little doubt as to the highlight of Willie Wallace's career or that of his team-mates on May 25, 1967 for that matter. He played a crucial part in the semi-final by netting the two vital goals against Dukla Prague.

His signing that season only reinforced an already potent goalscoring team and Lisbon wouldn't even have been in his mind when he started the season with Hearts.

A good pro and an easy-going man in the dressing room, Willie stamped his authority on that Celtic team, although he seemed to reserve his best performances for the crucial matches.

Aside from against Dukla Prague at Celtic Park on April 12,1967 in the semi-final of the European Cup when his brace help send the Bhoys to Czechoslovakia with a 3-1 lead, it was only four days later, in the Scottish Cup Final against Aberdeen, that he was on the spot to knock in the two goals which gave Celtic victory.

The bulk of the Lisbon Lions were at Celtic Park when Jock Stein arrived as manager, they just needed a few tweaks here and there. The last one in was Willie Wallace and the Big Man's jigsaw was complete – or was it?

It has been wrongly assumed that Willie was brought in to replace the injured Joe McBride but he was signed before the injury. It was far more likely that Stein may have been thinking of shuffling the side at the expense of the elder statesman of the attack, Stevie Chalmers – who went on to score the winner in Lisbon.

At any rate, Celtic weren't short of goals or goalscorers when Willie Wallace joined, but he still rattled in 21 goals over the remainder of that season to finish fourth behind Bobby Lennox on 24, Joe McBride on 35 and Stevie Chalmers on 36. That meant the top four scorers netted 117 goals of Celtic's 184-goal tally between them.

After five successful years at Celtic Park, Willie left for Crystal Palace in 1971, along with John Hughes.

WILLIE WALLACE
STRIKER
Celtic debut:
December 10, 1966, League, Celtic 4-2 Motherwell

	App	Subs	Goals
League	135	6	88
Scottish Cup	24	2	21
League Cup	31	5	12
Europe	27	2	13
Total	**217**	**15**	**134**

> **Wallace seemed to reserve his best performances for the crucial matches**

56 | MADE IN PARADISE

STORY OF OUR LEGENDS

PETER GRANT

1982 - 1997

On his first day at secondary school, Peter Grant was asked by a teacher where his future ambitions lay and the youngster replied without hesitation that he was going to play for Celtic. Even by that stage, Celtic were aware of his ability and he signed S-forms with the club aged 12. His progress through the ranks was sufficiently impressive to be awarded a professional contract with his boyhood heroes.

With a fair degree of football ability, allied to a will to win and an absolute devotion to the green and white Hoops, Peter Grant was destined to become a Celtic player, and the fact that only 18 men have played more games for the club throughout its history is a fact that will make him very proud.

Because Grant remains a supporter, in the same mould as his mentor and friend, the late, great Tommy Burns, someone who was lucky enough to play for the club he loved.

He provided the graft and grit in the Celtic midfield of the 1980s and early '90s, alongside the guile of Paul McStay, and then also John Collins.

Yet it would be wrong to say that was all Peter Grant brought to Celtic because you don't stay at Celtic for 15 years and make 478 appearances for the club if you're a bad player.

Talk about being thrown in at the deep end. Peter Grant made his full Celtic bow in a Glasgow derby as an 18-year-old in front of 40,000 fans at Ibrox on April 21, 1984, which was an indicator of Davie Hay's confidence in him. But it wouldn't be a dream debut for the midfielder as the home side took the spoils in a 1-0 victory thanks to a goal from Bobby Williamson 10 minutes after half-time.

Despite playing against 10 men for the remaining 30 minutes, the Hoops were unable to fashion an equaliser. It would prove a costly defeat as Celtic ended the season in second place behind Aberdeen, but Grant would enjoy further success during a long and distinguished career in Paradise.

Peter Grant's first major trophy arrived in 1986 as Celtic dramatically won the title on the last day of the season at Love Street. Although he wasn't on the pitch for that stunning 5-0 victory over St Mirren he was part of those incredible celebrations as the Hoops achieved the mother of all comebacks in Paisley.

Arguably, his most memorable moment in a Celtic jersey occurred in the double-winning centenary campaign. That was a fairytale 12 months in Paradise and Grant played a central role in the story, practically an ever-present in the side until a broken foot forced him to miss the last few games of the season, including the 1988 Scottish Cup final. He collected a Scottish Cup winner's medal the following year and was also awarded full international honours.

It wouldn't be until the 1995 Scottish Cup final win over Airdrie that Grant would get his hands on silverware again as Celtic ended their six-year trophy famine. Playing through the pain barrier, Grant was named Man of the Match for his magnificent efforts that day.

Peter Grant's desire and will-to-win won him the admiration of the Celtic support and he was recognised for his long years of service with a testimonial against Bayern Munich in 1997. More than 40,000 supporters crammed into Paradise to pay tribute to a player who always gave his all for the club and it was an emotional night for the midfielder and a fitting celebration of a devoted Celtic servant.

PETER GRANT

MIDFIELDER
Celtic debut:
April 4, 1984, League,
Rangers 1-0 Celtic

	App	Subs	Goals
League	338	26	15
Scottish Cup	34	4	1
League Cup	40	3	3
Europe	32	1	0
Total	**444**	**34**	**19**

58 | MADE IN PARADISE

WILLIE O'NEILL
1959 - 1969

Willie O'Neill was a key member of the Lisbon Lions' squad and played in the first four games of Celtic's run to European glory.

However, European football, never mind glory, seemed a long way off for the club and possibly nothing more than a pipedream as Willie realised his Bhoyhood ambition when he joined Celtic from St Anthony's on October 12, 1959.

He joined as a left-half after first developing his football skills just down the road from Celtic Park at the Sacred Heart while also playing for Our Lady of Fatima Boys' Guild before donning the green and white hoops at St Anthony's.

He signed on as an 18-year-old at Moorpark but the big Hoops at Celtic weren't slow off the mark when they became aware of his talents and he was still 18-years-old when he was snapped up by the only team he ever wanted to play for.

And although, after converting to full-back, it took him a couple of years to break through into the first team, he was to go on and feature in a couple of remarkable 'firsts' in the Hoops.

Not many players make their debut in a cup final but that's exactly what happened to the 20-year-old when he was thrust into the cauldron of a Scottish Cup final in 1961.

The game was, in fact, the replay following a 0-0 draw four days earlier with 113,328 watching and he took to the field in the Hoops for the first time in front of a crowd of 87,866.

The Celts lost that replay 2-0 but it was to a Dunfermline side managed by Jock Stein and once the Big Man returned to Celtic Park, he would be instrumental in Willie O'Neill racking up another couple of Celtic firsts.

On September 3, 1966 in a League Cup sectional 1-0 win over St Mirren at Love Street, he became Celtic's first ever substitute.

The day after that game, Jock Stein flew out to Switzerland to spy on Zurich and that led to another first for Willie when he was named in the starting XI for Celtic's first ever European Cup tie.

That first sub appearance also ensured that Willie played in every single one of Celtic's League Cup games that season – and that included his pivotal part in the final against Rangers on October 29.

He appeared from nowhere to clear a sure-fire Rangers 'goal' off the line in the final that Celtic won 1-0.

So his clearance was crucial in lifting the first trophy of Celtic's clean-sweep that season and a week later he played in another winning final as the second of the five trophies, the Glasgow Cup, was lifted.

However, by the turn of the year, Jock Stein had decided on his back two of Tommy Gemmell and Jim Craig Willie became a 'squad player' – a much-valued squad player.

He moved to Carlisle United in 1969 where injury forced him to retire in 1971 but there is no doubt where his heart lay and he will be forever known as Willie O'Neill of Celtic – Lisbon Lion.

WILLIE O'NEILL

FULL-BACK
Celtic debut:
April 26, 1961, Scottish Cup, Dunfermline 2-0 Celtic

	App	Subs	Goals
League	49	1	0
Scottish Cup	3	0	0
League Cup	18	2	0
Europe	9	0	0
Total	**79**	**3**	**0**

STORY OF OUR LEGENDS

MURDO MacLEOD

1978 - 1987

Mention the two league titles that Celtic won when the number 10 was significant, and Murdo MacLeod is a central character in both triumphs. In 1979, when '10 Men Won The League', he scored the final goal in Celtic's 4-2 victory over Rangers which secured the title in dramatic circumstances. And in 1998, when we 'Stopped the 10', he was assistant manager to Wim Jansen as another last-day drama unfolded at Paradise.

Murdo MacLeod was just 20-years-old when he joined Celtic, but he'd already garnered plenty of first-team experience at Dumbarton. And that paid immediate dividends for Celtic as he slotted into the midfield in what would prove to be a title-winning season under new manager, Billy McNeill.

He was strong and fearless in the centre of the park, with a tireless ability to keep running, and a ferocious shot that saw him score 82 goals for the club in nearly 400 appearances.

A much-loved player by the Celtic support, MacLeod became one of the few Scottish players to go and ply his trade abroad, joining Borussia Dortmund in 1987. And the three years he spent in Germany only further served to enhance his reputation. He even returned to Celtic Park when the German side drew Celtic in the first round of the 1987/88 UEFA Cup. MacLeod, not surprisingly, received a superb reception from the Celtic support.

Signing for the Hoops on November 2, 1978, Murdo MacLeod made his debut just two days later against Motherwell at Celtic Park but despite showing that he was an excellent signing, the 20-year-old couldn't help his new team to a win as they lost 2-1. On the whole, though, the season turned out not bad for a first term with the Celts as the young midfielder scored three goals in 27 games and the last of those goals was the Hoops' last of the season. It came in the last minute of the last game and helped the 10-man Celts not only to a historic 4-2 win over Rangers, but also to the championship on a never-to-be-forgotten May evening.

It was a Monday night in May 1979 when Celtic faced Rangers in the Hoops' final league campaign of a campaign which had been disrupted due to a harsh winter. The stakes were high, but also clear for Billy McNeill's side – victory over their city rivals would ensure that the league title returned to Paradise. Anything else and, with two more games remaining, the Ibrox side could have stole the title.

Rangers took a first-half lead and when Johnny Doyle was red-carded early in the second-half, things looked bleak for Celtic. However, the team produced a stunning performance and found themselves leading 3-2 going into the last minute. That's when Murdo MacLeod stepped forward.

That aforementioned game no doubt ranks highest in MacLeod's Celtic memories and it was the first, but by no means the last. He won no fewer than four championships with the club with titles in 1980/81, 1981/82 and 1985/86 following the first one in season 1978/79. The last of the four was also one to remember as it was another last-day, skin-of-the-teeth episode with MacLeod taking to the field in the 5-0 win at Paisley while Hearts were losing 2-0 to Dundee at Dens Park. There were also two Scottish Cup medals and a League Cup win for the tenacious midfielder.

MURDO MacLEOD

MIDFIELDER
Celtic debut:
November 4, 1978,
League,
Celtic 1-2 Motherwell

	App	Subs	Goals
League	274	7	55
Scottish Cup	36	2	7
League Cup	44	0	13
Europe	32	0	7
Total	**386**	**9**	**82**

60 | MADE IN PARADISE

LUBO MORAVCIK

1998 - 2002

LUBO MORAVCIK

MIDFIELDER
Celtic debut:
November 7, 1998,
League,
Celtic 6-1 Dundee

	App	Subs	Goals
League	75	19	29
Scottish Cup	9	1	1
League Cup	8	2	2
Europe	11	4	3
Total	**103**	**26**	**35**

Lubomir Moravcik's arrival at Celtic was met with indifference by the Scottish press. One columnist was moved to describe the transfer as "laughable" and label him as nothing more than one of Dr Jozef Venglos' "pals".

Yet after 90 mercurial minutes in his debut match against Dundee, which Celtic won 6-1, everyone realised that Celtic had a special talent on their hands. He was outstanding, with his sublime cross for Henrik Larsson's hat-trick goal the highlight of the match.

Costing just £300,000 from Duisburg, Moravcik immediately looked like the steal of the decade.

He had been a Celtic player for less than a month by the time Rangers arrived at Celtic Park for the first Glasgow derby of the 1998/99 season. It's a game that can make or break even seasoned professionals but Lubo was born for this stage.

Some 11 minutes had elapsed when he stepped on to Larsson's dummy and whipped an unerring left-foot finish into the bottom corner from 18 yards. Just four minutes into the second half, Lubo was at it again – powering home a bullet header to give Celtic a 2-0 lead. A Larsson double and a solitary Mark Burchill strike rounded off the famous 5-1 victory.

He maintained his love affair with the Glasgow derby in what is now known simply as the 6-2 game and it needs no real introduction. It was the first Glasgow derby of Martin O'Neill's reign and Celtic gave a signal of their intent in the Demolition Derby. Lubo was at the heart of it all. It was from his corner that Chris Sutton fired Celtic ahead, before Stilian Petrov met another expert Lubo delivery to make it 2-0. With Rangers all over the place, Lubo sold Barry Ferguson a dummy and cut the ball back to Paul Lambert for a stunning third. Larsson's double and Sutton's late goal sealed the win.

It carried on as Celtic travelled over the Clyde as champions in April 2001. Neil Lennon's pass was cushioned into Lubo's path by Larsson and the Slovakian curled his shot beyond Stefan Klos. Yet he wasn't finished. Running on to Shaun Maloney's flick, Lubo ghosted past Fernando Ricksen and again found the corner. Larsson's 50th goal of the season made it a dream afternoon for Celtic.

To single out these games, though, is a travesty as the skills of one of the greatest players to ever play for Celtic were a constant sight at grounds across Scotland and beyond. Lubo would trot over to take a corner and a band of Celtic fans would extend their arms and bow at the midfield genius. It was inspired by the 'We're Not Worthy' sketch from *Wayne's World* and this type of adulation meant a lot to Moravick, who always made sure he applauded the Hoops fans who idolised him.

The little magician scored 35 goals in his 129 games with 16 of those goals coming from his left foot, 16 from his right and three were headers and, in reference to trapping the ball with his backside against Hearts, the great man himself once said: "Football is not really about trapping the ball with your bum, though, it's about scoring goals and winning the game."

Few did that better than Lubo Moravcik.

STORY OF OUR LEGENDS

JOHN CLARK
1958 - 1971

John Clark is 'Mr Celtic'. He joined the club in 1958 as a 17-year-old, and has been involved with the club ever since. There have been occasional breaks in service, when he played or managed elsewhere, but Paradise always remained in his heart and it's where he always returned to.

He began life in the half-back line at Celtic, but was converted to a sweeper when Jock Stein returned to the club in 1965. And alongside Billy McNeill, Clark was part of a formidable defensive partnership that conquered all before them. Composed on the ball and with a great ability to read the game, John Clark was a crucial cog in Celtic's success, and he would later help deliver further success as assistant manager to Billy McNeill during the latter's first spell in charge at the club.

Lanarkshire Bhoy, Clark started with his local Chapelhall Boys' Guild before junior side, Larkhall Thistle were alerted to his talents in the left-half berth in October 1957. By the end of that season, Birmingham City were in the running for the youngster but no permanent deal was struck and Celtic's reserve coach, a certain Jock Stein, fielded Clark as a trialist on September 20. By October he was a fully-fledged Celtic player and joined a half-back line in the reserve side where he was partnered by Pat Crerand and Billy McNeill as the club's second string began to pick up plaudits – something that the first team were sadly lacking.

As one of the 'Kelly Kids' of the 1950s, Clark had been utilised at right-half when it was obvious that his natural berth was on the left-hand side of the defence but that all changed when Jock Stein arrived as manager in 1965. The new boss also adopted the sweeper system and Clark was the man for the job as Stein's Celts set about turning Scottish, not to mention European, football on its head. Between 1965 and 1971, Clark picked up four league championships, three Scottish Cups, four League Cups and, of course, the European Cup in 1967.

Between April 1965 and September 1967, Clark did not miss a single game for Celtic in any competition - 140 competitive Celtic games. During this time he also played four times for Scotland and Celtic played 17 major friendlies.

However, by 1968, injuries were beginning to take their toll and he was increasingly out of the side and this was perhaps the first indication that the Lisbon Lions weren't going to last forever on the field. Once the 1970s kicked in, the long-lasting servants were gradually departing and, as a dyed-in-the-wool Celtic supporter, Clark would not have enjoyed leaving the club in the least.

This was truly the end of an era as the final league of season 1970/71, a 6-1 home win over Clyde on May 1, was not only John Clark's last game for Celtic, it was also the last hurrah of the Lisbon Lions.

He returned to Paradise as a coach in 1973 and was Billy McNeill's right-hand man at both Aberdeen and Celtic. He was manager at Cowdenbeath, Stranraer, Clyde and Shotts Bon Accord before returning to Celtic as Kit Manager in the 1990s, meaning he worked at Celtic in the 1950s, '60s, '70s, '80s, '90s, 2000s and 2010s – a remarkable achievement.

JOHN CLARK

LEFT-HALF
Celtic debut:
October 3, 1959,
Scottish League,
Arbroath 0-5 Celtic

	App	Subs	Goals
League	185	1	1
Scottish Cup	30	1	1
League Cup	60	2	1
Europe	37	0	0
Total	**312**	**4**	**3**

62 | MADE IN PARADISE

JOHN CLARK

STORY OF OUR LEGENDS

BERTIE PEACOCK
1949 - 1961

Bertie Peacock spent less than a year at Coleraine before moving to Glentoran. He was there only slightly longer, though, and despite being on the books of consecutive Irish Cup final clubs (Coleraine in 1948 and Glentoran in '49) it was under rather more austere circumstances that he was spotted by Celtic scout Peter O'Connor.

It was after playing in the RUC Fives during the summer of 1949 that Celtic were alerted of his talents and he was on his way.

Bertie Peacock was also an illustration of Celtic's philosophy of being a club open to all, something that the founding fathers had been so determined to establish.

Born in Coleraine in 1928, he was from the Protestant community in the north of Ireland, but when Celtic signed him in 1948, it was further proof that Willie Maley's words – 'It is not his creed nor his nationality which counts - it's the man himself,' – were central to Celtic's identity.

It would be fair to say that his great friend, the inimitable Charlie Tully, wouldn't have been the kind of player he was if Bertie Peacock wasn't the kind of player Bertie Peacock was. That may sound like a bit of a conundrum but it is essentially simple and basically true. Indeed, both Tully and John McPhail nicknamed Bertie their 'labourer' such was his industrious input, and the great Jock Stein labelled him as 'a human dynamo' when the formidable half-back line of Evans, Stein and Peacock emerged in the mid-1950s.

His passing of the ball was excellent and a thunderbolt of a shot helped him amass 50 goals for the Celts.

He was no stranger to silverware. His first arrived at the end of his first season when the Bhoys beat Rangers 3-2 in the Charity Cup final known as the 'Danny Kaye Final' because of the Hampden appearance of the Hollywood superstar.

There had also been the Scottish Cup win of 1951 along with the St Mungo Cup, the Coronation Cup in 1953, the double of 1953/54 and the club's first League Cup win in 1956.

It was on the SS Mauretania as the Celts sailed to the States for a summer tour in 1957 that he was handed the captaincy and that League Cup win was to be repeated just a few months later – but with a rather more legendary outcome. Having only been skipper for a few months, Bertie led the team to their 7-1 League Cup final win over Rangers and highlights don't come much brighter than that.

Having captained Celtic to the 7-1 'Hampden in the Sun' League Cup triumph in October 1957, Bertie Peacock headed to Sweden at the end of the season as Northern Ireland took part in their first World Cup tournament. A victory over Czechoslovakia and a draw with West Germany was enough to reach the quarter-final, where they lost to France.

Peacock was a shining light in the tournament, and was nicknamed 'The Little Black Ant' by the local press because of his tireless running and the fact he seemed to be everywhere on the pitch.

BERTIE PEACOCK

LEFT-HALF
Celtic debut:
September 29, 1949,
League Cup,
Celtic 1-3 Aberdeen

	App	Subs	Goals
League	319	n/a	32
Scottish Cup	56	n/a	8
League Cup	80	n/a	10
Europe	n/a	n/a	n/a
Total	**455**	**n/a**	**50**

TOM BOYD
1992 - 2003

Tom Boyd enjoyed an exceptional playing career. He began life at Fir Park on a Youth Training Scheme and would go on to captain the side to Scottish Cup glory in 1991. He moved to Chelsea but soon returned to Scotland, joining his boyhood heroes. Boyd was at Celtic in the darkest days of the old board, and was a central figure as the club, and the team, re-emerged following Fergus McCann's takeover and Tommy Burns' appointment as manager.

He was in the side that won the Scottish Cup in 1995, the club's first trophy in six years, while he captained the team three years later when, under Wim Jansen, Celtic won the league and 'stopped the 10'. He also played his part in Celtic's treble success in 2000/01 under Martin O'Neill.

TOM BOYD
DEFENDER
Celtic debut: February 8, 1992, League, Celtic 2-0 Airdrie

	App	Subs	Goals
League	296	10	2
Scottish Cup	31	3	0
League Cup	31	2	0
Europe	33	1	0
Total	**391**	**16**	**2**

Tom Boyd is a genuine Celtic great, and another example of a supporter who was lucky enough to pull on the green and white Hoops. He might only have scored two goals for the Hoops, but he made over 400 appearances for the club, and he was a vital part of the Celtic team for 10 years.

Fortunately for Celtic, his stay at Chelsea was fairly short-lived. In what is still seen as one of the transfer deals of the decade, Celtic brought Boyd home in exchange for Tony Cascarino.

Alongside the midfield talent of Paul McStay and John Collins, Boyd would be at the heart of Celtic's triumph in 1995 as they lifted the Scottish Cup against Airdrie. The emotions displayed at the final whistle showed just what the win meant to all of the Celtic support – including Tom – ending a barren spell for the Bhoys that had lasted six years.

Tom Boyd was a consistent performer throughout his time at Celtic, and the disappointments he felt were as much as a supporter as a player. The early years of his time were frustrating, but he was also part of the resurgence of the club under Tommy Burns. And like his team-mates, his one regret is that they didn't win the title during Burns' tenure as manager.

Despite Celtic's inconsistent form during this period, Boyd would soon enjoy being at the heart of another major triumph for the Bhoys as the newly-appointed captain helped Wim Jansen's team stop the 10. Indeed he even had a helping hand in setting up Harald Brattbakk to seal the points against St Johnstone. While going on to play a part in the Bhoys' 5-1 and 6-2 victories over Rangers, perhaps his greatest achievement is being just the second

> Tom Boyd is a genuine Celtic great, and another example of a supporter who was lucky enough to pull on the green and white Hoops

captain in Celtic's history - after Billy McNeill - to captain the side to a treble in the 2000/2001 season.

On May 15, 2001, Alex Ferguson brought his Manchester United side to Celtic Park for a special occasion – a testimonial match for Tom Boyd in recognition of his faithful service to Celtic going back to when he joined the club in February 1992. The result of the game was a 2-0 victory for the English side, but it was still a night of celebration of a Celtic great. It's something that Tom Boyd appreciated and now, along with Billy McNeill and Davie Hay, he is a Celtic Football Club Ambassador.

STORY OF OUR LEGENDS

BOBBY EVANS

1944 - 1960

The early years of Bobby Evans' footballing career were spent around the South Side of Glasgow, initially with Sir John Maxwell's Primary and the Boys' Brigade then Maxwell Thistle and Thornliebank Methodist where a crunching tackle on Tommy Piltdown of Dumbarton saw the senior player recommend the young Evans to St Anthony's.

He signed for the Govan Hoops on January 24, 1944 but his performances in green and white at Moore Park soon caught the eye of the big team in the Hoops at the other end of the city. He signed for Celtic on July 23, 1944 just a week after his 17th birthday.

Although he signed for Celtic from St Anthony's while World War II was still raging on the continent, Evans didn't retire from the game until midway through the 1967/68 season at the age of 40.

The fact that Celtic had won the European Cup by that time was indicative of the changes made in the game since Bobby made his debut in the wartime Regional League against Albion Rovers.

Evans played a crucial part in the 1957 League Cup victory as Celtic ran Rangers ragged to record the highest scoreline in a major British cup final

A 10,000 crowd turned up at Albion Rovers' Cliftonhill and witnessed the debut of the teenage Evans in a game won 1-0 thanks to a penalty converted by the legendary Jimmy Delaney.

Until Danny McGrain started churning out Scotland appearances, Bobby was the most capped Celt with 45 of his 48 caps won at Celtic, though Evans always thought he should have gained more international recognition, and at one point in his career wrote to the SFA asking not to be considered for Scotland, a request he later retracted.

Evans' medal collection included three one-offs - The Victory in Europe Cup (1945), the St Mungo Cup (1951) and the famed Coronation Cup (1953). On the regular domestic scene he picked up winner's medals in the championship (1954), the Scottish Cup (1951 and 1954) and two League Cups (1956 and 1957).

It is the last of those trophy wins that will forever remain one of the most revered pages in any history books written about the club - the famous 7-1 League Cup victory over Rangers. Evans played a crucial part on that unforgettable day as Celtic ran Rangers ragged to record the highest scoreline in a major British cup final.

He had actually been the first Celtic captain to get his hands on the League Cup, raising it aloft in 1956 after the Hoops beat Partick Thistle 3-0 in a replay following a goal-less draw in the first final.

It was Celtic's first success since the 1938 league championship, and although he had relinquished the captaincy to Bertie Peacock by the time the Hoops retained the trophy with the demolition of Rangers the following season, it didn't diminish his delight at the triumph.

Evans, who was Fergus McCann's favourite Celtic player, moved to Chelsea in 1960, much to the dismay of the Celtic support, and following the spell at Stamford Bridge he moved on to Newport County, Morton, Third Lanark and Raith Rovers before finally hanging up his boots on December 14, 1967.

BOBBY EVANS

RIGHT-HALF, CENTRE-HALF
Celtic debut: August 19, 1944, Regional League, Albion Rovers 0-1 Celtic

	App	Subs	Goals
League	385	n/a	10
Scottish Cup	64	n/a	0
League Cup	88	n/a	1
Europe	n/a	n/a	n/a
Total	**537**	**n/a**	**11**
Wartime	14	n/a	1
Total	**551**	**n/a**	**12**

JIMMY McMENEMY

1902 - 1920

Within a couple of years of Jimmy McMenemy joining Celtic, the club embarked on a sustained period of dominance in Scottish football, and the man who could garner praise from all quarters, along with the nickname 'Napoleon', was central to that success.

He was Celtic's 'general', orchestrating the play and providing a creative spark that other teams found impossible to extinguish. He scored 164 goals for the club, a formidable total in itself, although that was only part of his contribution, and Jimmy Quinn's phenomenal goals tally of 217 owes much to Napoleon McMenemy.

It was on September 29, 1902 that Jimmy McMenemy made the first of his 516 appearances for Celtic, pulling on the green and white stripes to face Hearts at Celtic Park in a league match. The game finished in a 2-2 draw, with Johnny Campbell and Peter Somers scoring the goals for the Celts. It wouldn't be too long before McMenemy scored his first goal for the club, netting in a 3-0 victory over Port Glasgow Athletic towards the end of November.

The first of six consecutive league titles was delivered in 1905, although the destination of the title was only decided by a play-off between Celtic and Rangers at Hampden after both sides had finished level on points at the end of the season. Celtic won the game 2-1, with McMenemy scoring one of the goals, and the team were on the road to six-in-a-row.

He had also played in the Scottish Cup final triumph the previous season when a Jimmy Quinn hat-trick gave Celtic a 3-2 victory and their fourth success in the competition. It was also the club's first trophy success wearing their new green and white hooped kit that would, in the fullness of time, become one of the most famous and recognisable football strips in the world.

There were 11 league titles for McMenemy, with a solitary title in 1919 coming after the six-in-a-row and four-in-a-row successes. There were also six Scottish Cup triumphs with the Hoops, the first of which came in 1904 and the last some 10 years later, although he would later add another Scottish Cup winner's medal when he played in the Partick Thistle side that lifted the trophy with a victory over Rangers in the 1921 final.

In season 1919/20, Jimmy McMenemy had played in every game but one up until mid-February and didn't return until April when the Hoops played 11 games in 28 days, including a run of six games in 11 days. His final game came in the midst of all that when St Mirren visited on April 22, 1920.

He was a creative lynchpin in the side, and it was his skill on the ball, his ability to stay calm and collected, and his organisational prowess which earned him the nickname, 'Napoleon'. Those traits would be in evidence later in his career when he returned to Celtic Park as the club's trainer, helping to orchestrate further success for Celtic in the 1930s.

Jimmy McMenemy was one of those talents – one of the very best – and his importance to the team was never under-estimated by his manager, his team-mates or his fellow supporters, who appreciated what he did for the Celtic cause.

> **Jimmy's goals were only part of his contribution... he was Celtic's 'general', orchestrating the play and providing a creative spark that other teams found impossible to extinguish**

JIMMY McMENEMY

INSIDE-LEFT
Celtic debut:
September 29, 1902,
League,
Celtic 2-2 Hearts

	App	Subs	Goals
League	457	n/a	141
Scottish Cup	59	n/a	23
League Cup	n/a	n/a	n/a
Europe	n/a	n/a	n/a
Total	**516**	**n/a**	**164**

STORY OF OUR LEGENDS

JOHN HARTSON

2001 - 2006

Cast in the mould of an old-fashioned, classic British striker, John Hartson was the perfect foil for the lean and agile duo of Henrik Larsson and Chris Sutton when he was signed by Martin O'Neill in 2001.

Big and burly, Hartson offered a different approach for the Celts up front when the clever link-up play between Larsson and Sutton failed, but to pigeonhole the Welshman as an unskilful player would be unfair.

Hartson had enjoyed success at Arsenal, Wimbledon and Coventry, for a short spell, prior to moving to Celtic and he came with a price tag that matched his experience south of the border.

It took him a while to get off the mark in Scotland but when he eventually did, he was hard to stop.

The powerful forward finally found the net on his 11th appearance for the Celts, scoring a hat-trick in a league match against Dundee United on October 20 and he went on to finish his first year at Paradise with 24 goals in 35 starts.

Hartson continued in the same vein the following season but added goals in Europe to his name, the first of which came in an 8-1 victory over FK Suduva in the UEFA Cup.

The striker then netted an incredible four goals against Aberdeen in a 7-0 league rout at Paradise before scoring the decisive away goal in the second-leg of a nervy tie against Celta Vigo, which propelled the Bhoys into Europe past Christmas for the first time in 23 years.

The goals kept coming at home and abroad, including a wonderful long-range winner against Liverpool in the second-leg of the UEFA Cup quarter-finals at Anfield, but a back injury curtailed his season towards the close of the campaign and Hartson's year ended with a first-half goal against Celtic's city rivals in the Glasgow derby at the end of April.

The season ultimately concluded in disappointment for the rest of the team as well as they finished runners up in the league and UEFA Cup while also narrowly losing out in the League Cup final to Rangers.

Hartson's final two years under Martin O'Neill saw him remain Celtic's battering ram up front following the departure of Larsson to Barcelona and he scored a further 41 goals before breaking the 100 mark under new manager Gordon Strachan on November 6, 2005 in a match against Falkirk.

The faithful servant left the club in 2006 having won three league titles, two Scottish Cups and one League Cup but it was perhaps his victory over testicular cancer long after leaving Celtic that the humble Welshman will be most remembered for.

News of his condition came as a shock to the full football world when it was revealed in 2009, but particularly so the Celtic family, who had taken Hartson to their hearts during his time at the club.

True to form, however, the former Wales internationalist fought the disease to fully recover and founded the John Hartson Foundation, which aims to raise awareness of the condition and help those going through the same experience he did.

Big Bad John took cancer on much like he would any challenges on the pitch, and to this day is still regarded as a true fans' favourite by the Celtic support.

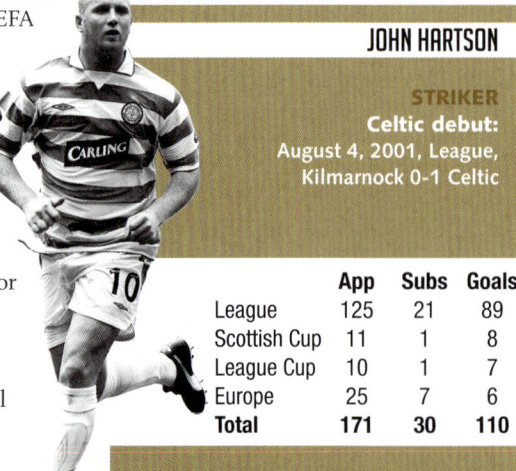

JOHN HARTSON
STRIKER
Celtic debut:
August 4, 2001, League,
Kilmarnock 0-1 Celtic

	App	Subs	Goals
League	125	21	89
Scottish Cup	11	1	8
League Cup	10	1	7
Europe	25	7	6
Total	**171**	**30**	**110**

FAMOUS FIVE

No.4 - Stopping the 10

It had been 10 long years since Celtic last won the championship in 1988 and there had been many changes during that time.

The players now had squad numbers and names of the back of their shirts, foreign imports were now the norm rather than the exception, Celtic were now a plc and a new all-seated stadium had all but risen from the ashes, the league had reverted to 36 games, we now had a General Manager and there had been FIVE 'real' managerial changes at Celtic Park…

Oh, and Rangers had won every one of the intervening nine titles – something had to be done!

The buck stopped at Fergus McCann and he could never be accused of trying to win popularity contests. It took a brave man to show fans' favourite Tommy Burns the door at such a crucial point in the club's history.

The relatively unknown Wim Jansen was the man who came in and Henrik Larsson wasn't the only new player. Marc Rieper, Regi Blinker, Stephane Mahe, Craig Burley, Paul Lambert, Darren Jackson, Jonathan Gould and Harald Brattbakk all joined the 'we-must-stop-the-10' club and all would

The 'we-must-stop-the-10' club all would play a role in the season to end all seasons

play a role in the season to end all seasons.

The championship campaign that had to be won at all costs couldn't have got off to a worse start. Hibernian won 2-1 on the opening day with new striker Henrik Larsson teeing up Celtic-daft Chic Charnley for the Easter Road winner. The following week was just as bad when Dunfermline won 2-1 at Celtic Park and the home crowd wouldn't witness Larsson's first goal in Paradise until a UEFA Cup match against Tirol Innsbruck – when he scored in his own net. The Celts then went on a winning run but a total of five league games were lost before the end of the calendar year – this wasn't going to be easy.

The championship challenge was the be-all and end-all and even the smoothest of bald heads sprouted a few grey hairs under the Celtic tammies when the Hoops challenge almost went 'bear-shaped' on the second-last weekend of the campaign at Dunfermline. The previous day, Kilmarnock's Ally Mitchell hit the winner in the 90th minute at Ibrox giving Celtic hope. The East End Park action was being beamed back to Celtic Park with the Hoops leading 1-0 thanks to a Simon Donnelly goal when a looping header from Craig Faulconbridge equalised with five minutes to go. Come May 9 cometh the Bhoys and this time Ibrox was hosting a beam-back from Tannadice while a helicopter was booked to fly the '10-in-a-row side' back to a packed stadium. However, the chopper got the chop. Dundee United 1-2 Rangers, Celtic 2-0 St Johnstone.

Larsson had opened the scoring early when he drifted in from the left before releasing a wonderful goal-bound shot from 22 yards.

The tension was unbearable, though, and the Celtic goal survived at least one scare in particular before, far too late in the second half for many, Tom Boyd played down the right to Jackie McNamara who squared the ball to Harald Brattbakk. The 10 was stopped!

STORY OF OUR LEGENDS

BILLY McNEILL
1957 - 1975

Billy McNeill has been a Celtic player, manager and ambassador. The man known simply as 'Cesar' captained the team during the golden era of the late 1960s and early '70s, winning nine league titles in a row, seven Scottish Cups and six League Cups. He also cemented his place as a Celtic legend on May 25, 1967 when he held aloft the European Cup in Lisbon's Estadio Nacional after leading the team to a 2-1 victory over Inter Milan.

He was a one-club man and, for Billy McNeill, that club had to be Celtic. He spent 18 years at the club, joining in 1957 and bowing out in 1975, and during that time he would make an incredible 790 appearances for his beloved Hoops, more than any other player in Celtic's long and illustrious history. Even more impressive is the fact that not one of those appearances was as a substitute. When Billy McNeill was fit, he played. It was as simple as that.

In much the same way as Jimmy McGrory's staggering haul of goals in Celtic colours is unlikely ever to be surpassed, the same can be true of Billy McNeill's appearances total, given that the era of the one-club player appears to have be consigned to football's history books.

It was with Our Lady's High School in Motherwell that McNeill first caught the eye of watching clubs, but there was only one club that he was destined to go to and that was Celtic. It is impossible to imagine Celtic without Billy McNeill and vice-versa.

Thankfully for Celtic fans, the club spotted his potential and he signed on August 20, 1957, immediately coming under the tutelage of then reserve coach, Jock Stein before being farmed out to junior side, Blantyre Vics. A year later to the exact day on August 20, 1958, Bobby Evans suffered a back injury in the opening league game against Clyde and that gave McNeill his chance.

He would become the rock upon which fortress Celtic Park was built, as the club emerged from the doldrums, and a

BILLY McNEILL

CENTRE-HALF
Celtic debut:
August 23, 1959,
League Cup,
Celtic 2-0 Clyde

	App	Subs	Goals
League	486	0	21
Scottish Cup	94	0	7
League Cup	138	0	4
Europe	72	0	3
Total	**790**	**0**	**35**

BILLY McNEILL

steadfast fulcrum around which everything evolved in the middle of the park. This man was the archetypal centre-half, towering majestically in the air to clear from defence or rising like a salmon to head home, often crucial, goals from corners. These were the skills that could be seen from the very back step of the terracing. What wasn't so obvious to the naked eye were his leadership qualities in harnessing those around him into a tight cohesive working unit that didn't know when they were beaten. His authority in the dressing room played as big a part in Celtic's success as his prowess on the park.

It was on May 3, 1975 that Billy McNeill pulled on Hoops for the 790th and last

time in a competitive match. Fittingly, it came in a cup final and ended with another piece of silverware as Celtic beat Airdrie 3-1 in the Scottish Cup final.

He returned as manager in 1978 and won three championships, a Scottish Cup and a League Cup before leaving to manage Manchester City and then Aston Villa. He returned north in time to lead Celtic to the centenary year Double and the following season lifted the Scottish Cup again.

His first league triumph as Celtic manager, back in 1979, remains one of the most incredible nights in the club's history, when the 10 men of Celtic beat Rangers 4-2 to secure the title.

MADE IN PARADISE | 71

STORY OF OUR LEGENDS

JOCK STEIN

1951 - 1957

Jock Stein is acknowledged as the finest manager Scotland has ever produced and it was Celtic's good fortune that he forged his reputation in the East End of Glasgow, and it's difficult to imagine how the club would have developed, or not, without the arrival of Stein as manager in 1965.

By then he had already established himself as a manager of considerable promise, having guided Dunfermline to a Scottish Cup triumph in 1961, when they beat Celtic, before moving to Hibernian.

But it was at Celtic Park that he truly made his reputation while, in turn, helping to make the modern-day Celtic.

He had a rather plain, even mundane, playing career – at one point swapping the minefields of Lanarkshire and Albion Rovers for the minefields of Wales and Llanelly.

That is, it was mundane until Celtic assistant trainer Jimmy Gribben, on the lookout for a mature player to help bring on the reserves, remembered 'something' about this cumbersome centre-half.

He signed in 1951, basically as fourth-choice centre-half and fate intervened when Stein suddenly found himself in the first team.

Not only did he keep his place but Lady Luck smiled on Celtic again when Sean Fallon suggested Stein be made captain – and so the mould was set.

Silverware followed in the shape of the Coronation Cup in 1953 and the league and Scottish Cup double the following year but fortune blew through Celtic Park once more when Stein was injured against, of all teams, Rangers.

That injury arrived on August 31, 1955 – just four days later on September 4, the very first European Cup game ever was played when the green and white hooped Sporting Lisbon took on Partizan Belgrade at the Estadio Nacional in Lisbon. You just couldn't make this stuff up.

Return from the ankle injury proved impossible and he turned to coaching the reserves – and this was true 'coaching', not mere training.

He persuaded the club to purchase the Barrowfield training ground and set about coaching the youngsters – many of whom who would come to fruition 10 years later in Lisbon.

Reserve football couldn't hold him though. He became manager at Dunfermline, with whom he beat Celtic in the cup final in 1961, and then Hibernian before the call came from Celtic Park once more in 1965.

What followed would have been deemed 'Fantasy Football' by the long-suffering Celtic support who faithfully stood by the men on the field during the barren years…

No fewer than **TEN** championships, nine of them all in a row, eight Scottish Cups and six League Cups but perhaps the most significant facet of Stein's Celtic was that they were feared throughout the length and breadth of Europe.

That was marked by the pinnacle of all that success when the Celts beat Inter Milan 2-1 in the European Cup final of May 25, 1967 in Lisbon.

The success was as astonishing as it was unexpected and still stands as the greatest period in the club's history.

There are three definitive eras in Celtic's history – the success-strewn decades of the early days, the years of decline and the return to glory – if it weren't for Jock Stein we could still very well be in the second phase and not knowing if we were ever going to get out of it.

JOCK STEIN

CENTRE-HALF
Celtic debut:
August 12, 1951,
League,
Celtic 2-1 St Mirren

	App	Subs	Goals
League	106	n/a	2
Scottish Cup	21	n/a	0
League Cup	21	n/a	0
Europe	n/a	n/a	n/a
Total	148	n/a	2

JOHN THOMSON

1926 - 1931

John Thomson signed for Celtic in 1926 at the age of 17, having been spotted playing for Wellesley Juniors by Celtic scout Steve Callaghan, who had also discovered Jimmy McGrory.

Celtic paid £10 for the young man who would go on to become known as the Prince of Goalkeepers, and by the age of 18 he had already made his first-team debut against Dundee at Dens Park in a 2-1 win for Celtic.

During his short time as Celtic goalkeeper, he won two Scottish Cup medals in 1927 and 1931.

International recognition followed on the back of his impressive displays and Thomson gained four caps for Scotland and four for the Scottish League.

A quiet and unassuming character off the park, once on the field of play Thomson had a natural athleticism aligned to a brave spirit and impressed all who had the privilege to see him play.

Sadly, those supporters who had quickly taken the young goalkeeper to their hearts would not enjoy watching his career develop and grow because his life was to end in the most tragic of circumstances on Saturday, September 5, 1931.

John Thomson received a serious head injury while playing against Rangers at Ibrox. He died later in hospital, having never regained consciousness after the incident.

The death of a footballer in his prime is thankfully rare, and even rarer on the field of play. Even after this length of time, John Thomson's untimely death at the age of just 22 remains one of football's great tragedies.

A young goalkeeper, already the first choice for his club and country, with a long and distinguished career seemingly ahead of him, dead as a result of an accident during a game.

Thomson was renowned for his bravery and fearlessness, and his dive at the feet of the Rangers forward Sam English as the player went to shoot was visible evidence of those virtues. As English shot, John Thomson's head took the full impact of the Rangers player's knee, leaving the goalkeeper unconscious and his head bleeding. He died later that same evening in hospital.

Thomson's death stunned football, and was particularly hard-felt by everyone connected with Celtic. Some 40,000 people attended the funeral in Cardenden, including thousands who had travelled through from Glasgow, many walking the 55 miles to the Fife village, and Thomson's coffin was carried by his devastated team-mates.

James Hanley, in his book *The Celtic Story* (1960) wrote: "It is hard for those who did not know him to appreciate the power of the spell he cast on all who watched him regularly in action. 'A man who has not read Homer,' wrote Bagehot, 'is like a man who has not seen the ocean. There is a great object of which he has no idea.'

"In like manner, a generation that

did not see John Thomson has missed a touch of greatness in sport, for which he was a brilliant virtuoso, as Gigli was and Menuhin is. One artiste employs the voice as his instrument, another the violin or cello. For Thomson it was a handful of leather. We shall not look upon his like again."

The final thought on the tragic events of September 1931 is to remember the epitaph on John Thomson's gravestone, which reads: 'They never die who live in the hearts they leave behind.'

JOHN THOMSON

GOALKEEPER
Celtic debut:
February 12, 1927,
League,
Dundee 1-2 Celtic

	App	Subs	Goals
League	163	n/a	0
Scottish Cup	25	n/a	0
League Cup	n/a	n/a	n/a
Europe	n/a	n/a	n/a
Total	**188**	**n/a**	**0**

MADE IN PARADISE | 73

STORY OF OUR LEGENDS

TOMMY GEMMELL
1961 - 1971

There are very few players can boast of scoring in a European Cup/Champions League final. There are even fewer who can say they've done it twice. Tommy Gemmell is one such player who can.

He scored Celtic's equaliser in the 1967 final in Lisbon as the Hoops went on to win the trophy with a 2-1 win over Inter Milan. Three years later, he opened the scoring the final at the San Siro Stadium in Milan, but this time it was Celtic who lost out as Feyenoord secured a 2-1 extra-time victory.

One of the players who arrived at the club courtesy of Sean Fallon, Tommy Gemmell would go on to establish himself as one of the best full-backs in the club's history, while his scoring exploits saw him net a total of 63 goals in his Celtic career, including those two European Cup final goals, which is a very impressive return for a defender.

In the early 1960s, Celtic had opted to pursue a policy of developing their own players and bringing them through the ranks and into the first-team. There was certainly short-term frustration for supporters, who were starved of any tangible success since the 1957 League Cup final triumph over Rangers, but in the longer-term it was a policy which struck gold.

Before initially settling as a right-back, Tommy Gemmell originally played on the right wing when he was at school. He then moved to left-back where he tried out on that side of defence at his amateur club, Meadow Thistle – mainly because they were short in players for that position.

It was late October 1961 when 17-year-old Gemmell eventually signed for Celtic, and he did so from Junior club, Coltness United.

A lot of hard work finally paid off two years later when Tommy Gemmell was eventually handed the chance to make his debut in the green and white Hoops. It came on January 5, 1963 in a league match against Aberdeen at Pittodrie. The trip north was a successful one at that, as Celtic wrapped up a 5-1 win against the Dons thanks to a John Hughes hat-trick and a Bobby Craig brace.

At Lisbon, he scored the equalising strike on 62 minutes, which brought Celtic back into the match. Stevie Chalmers then added a second five minutes from the end, and the rest they say, is history. Gemmell was also the first Celtic player to score in the European Cup – hitting home against FC Zurich in September 1966.

His last run-out for Celtic came on November 3, 1971 when the Hoops beat Sliema Wanderers 2-1 in the second round of the European Cup.

He moved to Nottingham Forest, but having returned to Scotland, Gemmell was captain of Dundee when they reached the League Cup final in 1973. Not surprisingly, they faced Celtic in the final, and on a day when the sun definitely didn't shine at Hampden, it was the dark blue side who triumphed, winning 1-0. And it was Gemmell as captain, who led the team up to lift the trophy.

Tommy Gemmell scored 63 goals for Celtic, and 31 of them came from the penalty spot. Indeed, he only ever missed three penalties throughout his Celtic career, and with a ferocious shot, it's no wonder goalkeepers had difficulty in saving them.

TOMMY GEMMELL

FULL-BACK
Celtic debut:
January 5, 1963, League, Aberdeen 1-5 Celtic

	App	Subs	Goals
League	247	0	38
Scottish Cup	43	0	3
League Cup	74	0	10
Europe	54	0	12
Total	**418**	**0**	**63**

TOMMY GEMMELL

There are very few players can boast of scoring in a European Cup final. There are even fewer who can say they've done it twice. Tommy Gemmell is one such player who can

STORY OF OUR LEGENDS

WILLIE MALEY
1888 - 1897

A talented half-back, Willie Maley played a total of 96 competitive games for Celtic between 1888 and 1897, scoring four goals.

He signed from Third Lanark after starting out with junior side Cathcart Hazlebank. Born in Newry, Ireland, Willie was a talented athlete who caught the eye of the Celtic committee immediately.

In 1892, when Celtic won their first Scottish Cup, he was an inspirational figure in the side. It would be a sign of things to come. Maley officially retired when he took on the role of manager, but pulled on his boots and the Celtic strip one last time on an emergency basis during a European tour in 1904.

He was Celtic's only manager in the first 50 years of the club's history although it would be inaccurate to suggest he was in the hot seat for the full half century.

Maley was, though, one of the cornerstones around which the club was built and it's difficult to imagine Celtic being the institution they are without his single-minded input.

He joined with the very first batch of founding players in 1888 and six years later became player/secretary while the team was still picked by the Match Committee.

Back on May 28, 1888, when Celtic played their first-ever game, the line-up for the match included a young Willie Maley, who started in midfield against Rangers. It's fitting that he was there from the start, considering the influence he would go on to have at the club over the next 50 years. Celtic won the match 5-2 and Maley played his part. Neil McCallum scored the first Celtic goal and went on to grab a double in that game. Tom Maley, Willie's brother, was credited with a hat-trick in some quarters. The first page of Celtic's history had been written.

In 1897 on the formation of the Limited Liability Company he took up the post of secretary/manager, but it's thought that his powers over team selection were restricted until the years between the wars when he took on the mantle of the more modern-day manager.

The Scottish Cup and the championship (three times) had already been won before he grasped the managerial reins but the addition of another 16 titles and 14 Scottish Cups set the benchmark and made Celtic the club they are today – and like all true Celtic management greats, he started his tenure off by lifting the title in his first season.

A total of 14 Glasgow Cups and 19 Charity Cups among others like the Empire Exhibition trophy helped take his trophy tally as manager to 68.

He was at the helm for close to 2,000 games and that incredible record of one of the greatest managers football has ever seen will surely never be surpassed.

In August 1953 Celtic played Irish side

WILLIE MALEY

Bohemians in a testimonial match for Willie Maley and the Hoops won 10-1. The game was arranged to allow Celtic supporters to honour the career of Maley, but he didn't just pocket the £2,000 that was raised for him – instead he gave the money to charity, or more specifically, to the Grampian Sanatorium in Kingussie.

He passed away in Glasgow in 1958 just three weeks short of his 90th birthday and, in truth, it would take Celtic 25 years from the time of his retirement to replace him with a figurehead of similar stature and man-management qualities when Jock Stein arrived.

It was only the arrival of Celtic's next 'Big Man' that the trophy haul started to emulate that of Maley's golden years when his Bhoys created a then world record by lifting the title six years in a row.

> Back on May 28, 1888, when Celtic played their first ever game, the line up for the match included a young Willie Maley, who started in midfield against Rangers. It's fitting that he was there from the start, considering the influence he would go on to have at the club over the next 50 years

WILLIE MALEY

HALF-BACK
Celtic debut: May 28, 1888,
Inaugural Match,
Celtic 5-2 Rangers

	App	Subs	Goals
League	75	n/a	2
Scottish Cup	25	n/a	2
League Cup	n/a	n/a	n/a
Europe	n/a	n/a	n/a
Total	**96**	**n/a**	**4**

MADE IN PARADISE | 77

STORY OF OUR LEGENDS

JIMMY QUINN

1900 - 1915

Jimmy Quinn's love of his hometown of Croy never faltered and he had to be cajoled into joining Celtic from the local Smithston Albion when he didn't want to travel into far away Glasgow by train, but sign he did, and on the last day of 1900 he joined his one and only professional club.

That signature was as a provisional but, just a week after fully signing as a professional, he made his debut on January 19, 1901 when Celtic travelled to St Mirren and the youngster scored in a 4-3 victory. That was the first of 217 goals in 331 games for Celtic up until he retired from the playing side of the game in 1915.

It was the 1904 Scottish Cup final that made him. This was the first Scottish Cup final to be played at the redeveloped Hampden Park in front of a massive 65,000 – and it was the first one in which Celtic wore their new style of jersey – the Hoops.

Rangers were 2-0 ahead and looked well on top of a lacklustre Celtic team. But it was Quinn who led the fight-back and his feat of scoring a hat-trick in a Scottish Cup final wasn't emulated by anyone until Dixie Deans repeated the trick for Celtic against Hibernian in 1972.

He had started, though, on the left wing but manager Willie Maley moved him into the middle and in one of his earlier games there, he scored a hat-trick against Rangers in the final of Glasgow Exhibition Trophy and that obviously whetted his appetite for netting triples in derby finals against the club's biggest rivals.

When added to that Glasgow Exhibition Trophy, five Glasgow Cup wins and four Charity Cup gongs gave him no fewer than **TEN** winning medals in the era's so-called more minor trophies but even that was surpassed in the ones that really matter.

He picked up **ELEVEN** top trophies, six championships (all in a row) and five Scottish Cups in an amazing career with the club. He established himself as a Celtic legend, one of the best goalscorers ever to wear the green and white hoops (and stripes too, since he joined the club in 1900, three years before the Hoops were adopted).

Indeed, there are only four players who have scored more goals for Celtic than Jimmy Quinn – Stevie Chalmers (231), Henrik Larsson (242), Bobby Lennox (277) and Jimmy McGrory (468) – and three of those men played in the post-Second

> **Quinn is one of the best goalscorers ever to wear the green and white hoops (and stripes too, since he joined the club three years before the Hoops were adopted)**

World War era, with League Cup ties and European fixtures added to the league and Scottish Cup.

As his career reached the autumn years, the injuries were taking longer to recover from and a knee injury in particular was causing him particular trouble. In his last couple of seasons he only appeared in the team sporadically and it was on January 30, 1915 that he played his last game in the Hoops. Hearts were the visitors on league duty and Andy McAtee got the goal in a 1-1 draw watched by 45,000 with 10,000 of the crowd in uniform because of the First World War.

His final goal was scored on Boxing Day, 1914 when Hamilton Accies lost 3-1, one of four he scored in six appearances to add to two goals he scored in only one league appearance the previous season. Celtic lifted the title in his last two seasons but his appearances tallies fell short of picking up a medal.

When he finally did hang up his boots on January 30, 1915, he returned to the coalface once more – something he had seemingly always planned on. He returned to Croy but still made the trip into Paradise for every game – this time as a supporter.

JIMMY QUINN

CENTRE-FORWARD
Celtic debut:
January 19, 1901,
League, St Mirren 3-4 Celtic
(scored once)

	App	Subs	Goals
League	273	n/a	187
Scottish Cup	58	n/a	30
League Cup	n/a	n/a	n/a
Europe	n/a	n/a	n/a
Total	**331**	**n/a**	**217**

CHARLIE GALLAGHER

1958 - 1970

Despite playing with Kilmarnock Amateurs, not even the persuasive powers of Willie Waddell at Rugby Park could make Charlie Gallagher sign for the club once Celtic's name was in the hat.

Gallagher would remain at Celtic for over a decade as the club was transformed from perennial underachievers into one of best teams in the world under Jock Stein.

During that era, the silky midfielder would make a massive contribution to those achievements in the greatest Hoops side ever assembled, and narrowly missing out on a place in the European Cup final in Lisbon.

Between 1958 and 1970, he played in 171 matches and scored 32 goals, picked up Scottish Cup, League Cup and League medals, as well as two Irish caps. Yet, his name will live on among the Celtic support mainly for two specific corners.

The first of these came against Dunfermline in the Scottish Cup final on April 24, 1965. With eight minutes to go, the teams were locked at 2-2, when Celtic were awarded a corner out on the left. Charlie ambled over to take it,

> **Gallagher would remain at Celtic for over a decade - the silky midfielder would make a massive contribution to the greatest Hoops side ever assembled**

sent a beautiful ball into the middle and Billy McNeill rose above everyone else to power the ball home for the winner – the Celtic glory years begun in that instant.

Just under two years later, against Vojvodina in the quarter-final of the European Cup, as Celtic approached the final whistle locked on 1-1, they won another of the many corners that night, this time out on the right.

A play-off in Rotterdam looked likely and Charlie was about to place a short corner to Jimmy Johnstone – until he saw two markers being drawn out of the area. In an instant he changed his mind and sent a beautiful out-swinger into the box and once again Billy McNeill avoided the crowd in the area and rose to head home another winner – Lisbon was back on the agenda.

It was apt has he had played in Celtic's first ever European game when they were give a baptism of fire against Valencia in 1962, and it was the start of an incredible journey for the club.

Within the caldron of the Mestalla Stadium, the Hoops lost 4-2, a credible result, particularly given the disruption they encountered prior to the game.

Despite Gallagher and his team-mates' best attempts, however, they couldn't manage to overturn that deficit in Glasgow, with the return fixture finishing in a 2-2 draw, consigning them to an early exit from the tournament.

A gifted Valencia side went on to retain their trophy, while Celtic proved quick learners in this environment, reaching the last four of the Cup-Winners' Cup the following season. Just four years later, they were champions of Europe under the masterful guidance of Jock Stein.

Gallagher made a vital contribution to that stunning success and the classy midfielder played his part in a host of other European encounters during a 12-year career with his beloved Hoops.

A cousin of Paddy Crerand, he also became the first Scotland-born player to represent the Republic of Ireland and, to celebrate that, Jock Stein allowed him to lead the Celts out as captain in the Scottish Cup against Elgin City in February, 1967.

CHARLIE GALLAGHER

INSIDE-FORWARD
Celtic debut:
August 22, 1959,
League Cup,
Celtic 1-0 Raith Rovers

	App	Subs	Goals
League	107	0	17
Scottish Cup	23	0	4
League Cup	28	0	11
Europe	13	0	0
Total	**171**	**0**	**32**

STORY OF OUR LEGENDS

HENRIK LARSSON

1997 - 2004

He would go on to score 242 goals in 315 appearances, making him Celtic's third top goalscorer of all time - the list of Henrik's achievements at Celtic could go on forever

Henrik Larsson arrived at Celtic Park in 1997 without too much of a fanfare. He left seven years later, heralded as one of the club's greatest ever players. He was the Super Swede, the Magnificent Seven, the King of Kings. He was Henrik Larsson of Celtic, and supporters loved him.

The Swedish striker joined Celtic from Feyenoord, signed by his former manager, Wim Jansen, following protracted contract difficulties with the Dutch club.

It's well-documented that one of his first touches as a Celtic player was to set up Chic Charnley to score the winning goal for Hibernian in a 2-1 loss at Easter Road, yet he would go on to score 242 goals in 315 appearances, making him Celtic's third top goalscorer of all time, behind only Bobby Lennox and Jimmy McGrory.

He scored his first goal for the Hoops in his second match – a 7-0 win over Berwick Rangers in the League Cup, and in that first season he would end up with 19 goals and two winner's medals, including a league medal as Celtic 'stopped the 10'.

The list of Henrik's achievements at Celtic could go on forever. He won four

SPL titles, two League Cups, two Scottish Cups, and he was the top goal scorer in the Scottish Premier League in five out of six seasons. In season 2000/01, Martin O'Neill's first in charge at the club, Henrik had one of his most successful seasons at the club. He scored an incredible 35 league goals in 38 league matches, with an overall total of 53 goals in the season, helping Celtic win the treble. On a personal level, he also won the European Golden Shoe as the continent's top scorer.

Celtic began to dominate Scottish football and re-establish themselves as a European force and, not surprisingly, their Super Swede was at the heart of the success. His goals on the road to Seville were absolutely vital, and he produced a stunning performance in the 2003 UEFA Cup final, scoring two goals.

The main low points of his time at the club were the broken leg he suffered in 1999 and, later, the heartache of the UEFA Cup final where, despite an extraordinary performance which included two goals, he saw Porto lift the trophy with a 3-2 win after extra-time.

He left Celtic in the summer of 2004 for Barcelona, after seven sensational years at the club. His final game at Paradise was a league clash against Dundee United, where naturally he scored both goals to give Celtic a 2-1 victory. During his last competitive appearance for the Hoops, he scored another two goals to help Celtic beat Dunfermline and win the Scottish Cup. There was to be one final bow at Paradise – a farewell game against Sevilla – when the Celtic support said thank you and goodbye to the Magnificent Seven.

There was to be another appearance at Celtic Park in the colours of Barcelona the following season. Not surprisingly, he scored in the 3-1 victory for the Catalan giants.

HENRIK LARSSON
FORWARD
Celtic debut:
August 3, 1997,
League,
Hibernian 2-1 Celtic

	App	Subs	Goals
League	218	3	174
Scottish Cup	25	0	23
League Cup	11	0	10
Europe	58	0	35
Total	**312**	**3**	**242**

80 | MADE IN PARADISE

HENRIK LARSSON

FAMOUS FIVE

No.5 - Birthday Bhoys beat the best in the world

The day after Celtic celebrated their 125th anniversary, Victor Wanyama and Tony Watt wrote another page into the club's history books, scoring the goals which beat Barcelona 2-1 in the UEFA Champions League.

After an outstanding performance for 94 minutes, the Hoops kept the greatest team in the world at bay, and even an injury-time strike by Lionel Messi wasn't enough to stop them taking all three points.

It was one of the most incredible European nights ever seen at Paradise, and one of the most stunning results in the history of the UEFA Champions League.

And after a magnificent stadium display celebrating the 125th anniversary, Barcelona got the game underway amid an electric atmosphere. It took a while for the game to settle, with play sweeping frantically from end to end, but neither side troubled the goalkeeper in the opening stages.

Celtic put Barcelona under pressure on 20 minutes when Wanyama made a break through the centre of the pitch and even though possession was lost, he won it back excellently just seconds later.

Teaming up with Ambrose, the defender won the Hoops a corner and from it they took the lead. Charlie Mulgrew swung it to the back post, and jumping above everyone, Wanyama, the stand-out performer of the opening period, headed it into the net.

And as if the atmosphere wasn't thunderous enough, Paradise erupted, and continued to be a cauldron of noise as the match got back underway.

Celtic continued to push forward, and came within inches of doubling their advantage six minutes later. From the left flank Adam Matthews played the ball through to Samaras, who beat the offside trap, but Victor Valdes intercepted the cross before the Greek could slot it into the net.

Barcelona were keen to respond quickly and looked confident moving forward. Lionel Messi cracked an effort off the bar on the half-hour mark, but Fraser Forster looked to have got his fingertips to it, and did well to save the shot.

With the visitors continuing to put pressure on Celtic, they hit the woodwork again, this time through Alexis when he met Dani Alves' ball, and sent it crashing off the far post. It was the last real chance on target inside the first-half, though, and the Hoops went into the break enjoying the one-goal lead.

Barcelona came out strong in the second period and won a string of corners, but good defending, especially from Matthews, kept them at bay. And on the hour mark Forster continued the good work with a double save, keeping Alexis out with his hands and then his legs.

Celtic had the chance to extend their advantage on 64 minutes when Mulgrew took advantage of a defensive mix-up and found himself in space, but he couldn't get the final touch to bundle the ball past Valdes.

Forster continued excel at the opposite end of the pitch, and pulled off a series of world-class saves to deny the Catalan giants. They responded by bringing on World Cup winners David Villa, Cesc Fabregas and Gerard Pique but they still couldn't break Celtic down.

And it was another Forster's outstanding block, and clearance, which set up Celtic's second. The ball forward deceived Xavi and with a blistering run into the box, substitute Watt became a hero as coolly slotted the ball past Valdes to make it 2-0.

There was only seven minutes left to play but Celtic Park was already in party mode, raising the roof with their celebrations.

Four minutes of stoppage were added, and in typical Barca style they weaved their way through Celtic and completed a sublime passing display with a goal. Messi latched on to the loose ball after another great Forster save, and made it a nervy end for the home support.

But it was too little too late for Barcelona and a momentous victory was sealed for Neil Lennon's side.

JOHNNY CRUM
1932 - 1942

Johnny Crum joined Celtic from Ashfield Juniors in February, 1932 and immediately joined a talented reserve side that also included Malky MacDonald and John Divers and he made his debut later that year by scoring twice in a 4-1 home win over Motherwell.

His debut in the No.9 position arrived in the absence of the injured Jimmy McGrory but it wasn't until the following season that he became a regular in the side in the No.7 role.

Season 1934/35 was a quiet one for him but the following term he played in every single game and picked up championship and Charity Cup medals.

During that campaign, the Celts beat Rangers 2-1 at Ibrox, their first win there for 14 years but it should be remembered that teams only played home and way once each in those days – and there were five drawn games in that sequence. Frank Murphy and Johnny Crum got the all-important goals as the Celts went on to lift the league title that season

That was the start of a silver-laden few seasons for the player and he took up the goal-scoring challenge when McGrory retired in 1937.

That run of medals included the championships of 1936 and 1938, the Scottish Cup of 1936/37, the Charity Cup in 1935/36 and 1937/38, the Glasgow Cup in 1938/39 and, significantly, the Empire Exhibition Trophy in 1938.

There was also another Glasgow Cup thrown in for good measure during the war years in 1940/41.

He also had the distinction of, on January 22, 1938 in a 2-1 Scottish Cup win over Third Lanark at Cathkin, scoring Celtic's 4,000th competitive goal.

His most revered goal, however, came in the tournament was organised to mark the Empire Exhibition being staged in Glasgow's Bellahouston Park and all of the games were played at nearby Ibrox.

The Celts, along with Rangers, Aberdeen and Hearts, represented the best of Scotland with Everton, Chelsea, Sunderland and Brentford travelling north as the best teams from England.

On June 10, Celtic and Everton lined up in front of 82,000 to contest this 'British Championship' as the final was billed, and it took until extra-time for the deciding goal to arrive.

JOHNNY CRUM
FORWARD
Celtic debut:
October 22, 1932, League, Celtic 4-1 Motherwell (scored twice)

	App	Subs	Goals
League	190	n/a	73
Scottish Cup	21	n/a	14
League Cup	n/a	n/a	n/a
Europe	n/a	n/a	n/a
Total	**211**	**n/a**	**87**
Wartime	69	n/a	23
Total	**280**	**n/a**	**110**

It was Johnny Crum who netted the all-important counter seven minutes into the extra period and he blazed something of a trail by celebrating with a wee dance behind the goal – exhibitionism that was unheard of in 1938 and in more than one paper the following day, he was chastised for 'over-celebrating'.

However, he may have been celebrating his entire input for the tournament as he scored the equaliser in Celtic's 3-1 win over Sunderland and netted the only goal of the game in the semi-fnal victory over Hearts prior to putting the ball past Everton's Ted Sagar in the final.

Johnny Crum got married on the morning of June 15, 1938. In the afternoon he was at the City Chambers along with his team-mates to receive the Charity Cup and in the evening he was at the Grosvenor Restaurant as a guest at the club's 50th Anniversary celebrations – all this coming just days after he had scored the winning goal in the Empire Exhibition Trophy final against Everton.

His Celtic story could have been even greater had it not been for the interruption of the Second World War and in 1942 he moved to Morton where he teamed up once more with fellow former Celt, John Divers.

STORY OF OUR LEGENDS

SCOTT BROWN

2007 to date

By holding the Scottish Premiership prize aloft for the fifth time in a row, Brown became the first captain of the club to so since Billy McNeill

Scott Brown was the hottest property in Scottish football, with a price tag to match, when Celtic made their move for the then 21-year-old in the summer of 2007.

Combative, dynamic and full of enterprise, the midfielder had been at the heart of a vibrant and entertaining Hibernian side since emerging from the club's youth ranks at just 17.

His impressive performances had earned him plenty of suitors on both sides of the border, but Gordon Strachan managed to persuade the Fifer that his future lay in Paradise. He calls this 'the best decision I have ever made'.

In the intervening years, Brown has overcome personal tragedy, several serious injury set-backs and a number of managerial changes to become a great Celtic servant and one of the club's most successful captains.

His first season ended with a silver lining as Celtic completed an incredible comeback to lift a third successive title on the last day of the season away to Dundee United, but the illness and then tragic passing of his little sister Fiona, along with the devastating loss of Tommy Burns, meant it was a bittersweet moment for him.

Demonstrating real strength of character, he bounced back in the following season to become Scotland's Player of the Year and help the Hoops lift the League Cup, though this time there was collective disappointment as the team fell narrowly short in the championship battle to Rangers on the last day of the season.

There were more mixed fortunes for Brown as the Tony Mowbray era got underway. Sidelined for much of the campaign through injury, he could only watch on frustrated as the team's form fluctuated and they fell further behind in the title race.

However, before Mowbray departed the club in March 2011, he bestowed the captaincy on Brown on the midfielder's return from injury. This move was a surprise to many at the time given the Dunfermline-born player's jocular nature off the pitch but he relished the additional responsibility and quickly proved any doubters wrong.

Having proved his leadership skills during a turbulent time for the club, he retained the armband under Neil Lennon, leading Celtic to Scottish Cup success, with the league, once again, just eluding the Bhoys on the last day of the campaign.

It was also during these 12 months that the 'Broony' celebration was born after he curled home a stunning equaliser in a Glasgow derby at Ibrox, a moment that further endeared him to the Celtic support.

Brown was Neil Lennon's undisputed general on the pitch as Celtic regained supremacy in Scotland and won three titles in a row, along with another Scottish Cup. He also played a crucial role as the Hoops reached the last 16 of the UEFA Champions League.

At several times in this period, he played through the pain barrier, inspiring those around him with his sheer will to win and unwavering commitment to the cause.

His growing maturity and authority on the pitch was underlined in February 2013, when Brown was appointed skipper of the national team by his former Celtic boss Gordon Strachan. He has now amassed over 50 caps for his country, earning him a place in the SFA Roll of Honour.

Further success followed for Brown at club level after Ronny Deila took over the reins in 2014. The league and League Cup were secured in the Norwegian's first season in charge and Brown crowned off the next campaign by holding the Scottish Premiership prize aloft for the fifth time in a row, becoming the first captain of the club to so since Billy McNeill.

As he heads into his 10th year as a Celt under new manager Brendan Rodgers, Brown will be aiming to add to his six league championships, two Scottish Cups and two League Cups at the place he now calls home.

SCOTT BROWN

MIDFIELDER
Celtic debut:
August 5, 2007, League,
Celtic 0-0 Kilmarnock

	App	Subs	Goals
League	236	14	24
Scottish Cup	17	2	2
League Cup	29	2	7
Europe	62	2	1
Total	**344**	**20**	**34**

(Stats correct up to end of season 2015/16)

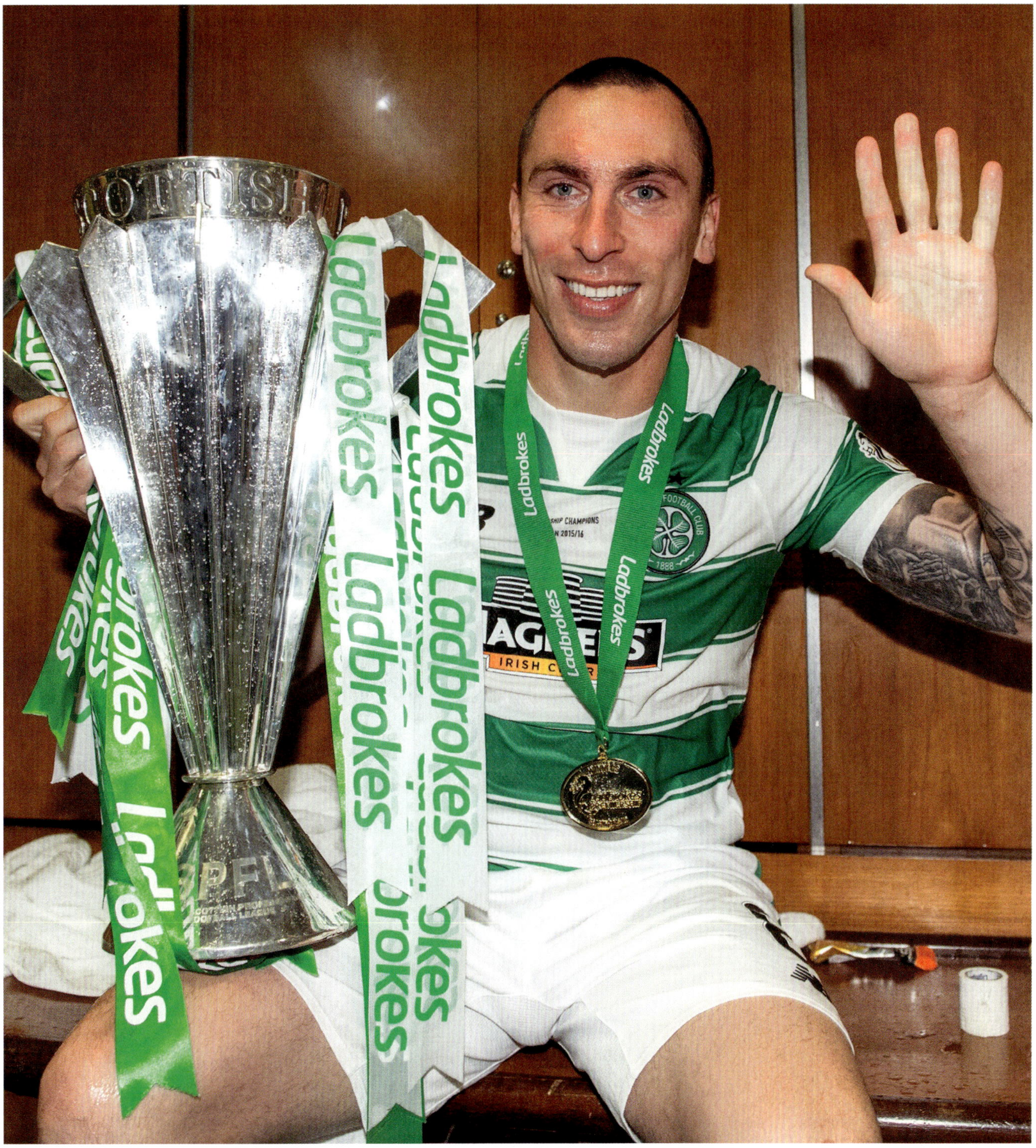
Ladbrokes
Ladbrokes
Ladbrokes
IRISH CIDER

CARLING
BROWN
8

MAGNERS

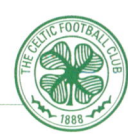

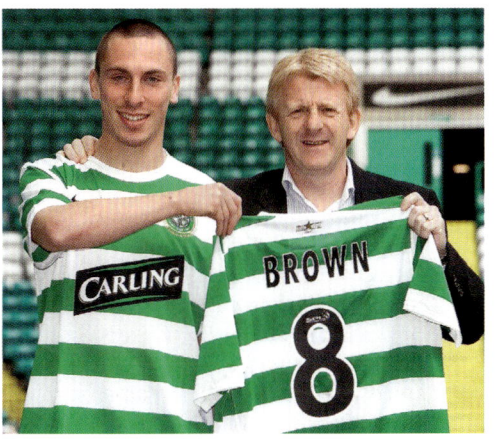

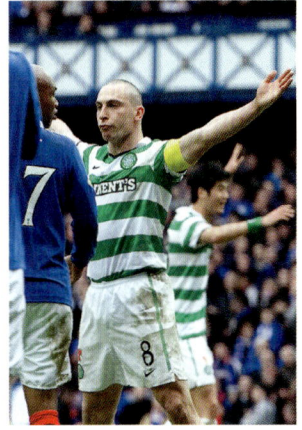

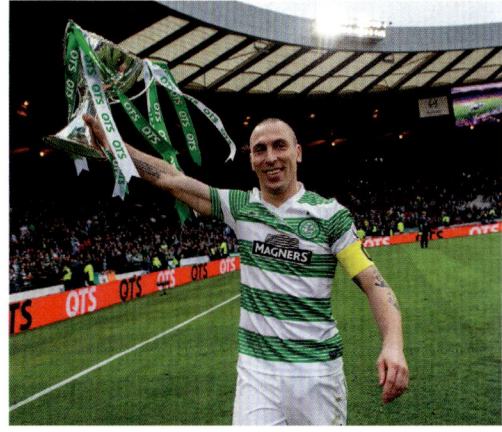

STORY OF OUR LEGENDS

TOMMY BURNS
1973 - 1989

Tommy Burns always described himself as a supporter who got lucky. Yet, in truth, it was the Celtic support who considered themselves lucky enough to have seen him play. He played 503 times for Celtic, always proud to wear his beloved green and white Hoops. His passion for the club was there for all to see, and he was always viewed by fans as one of their own, someone who, if he hadn't been blessed with such football talent, would have been standing in The Jungle cheering on the team.

He had a rather short road to Paradise as he lived not far along the road in the Calton district of Glasgow, and the draw of Celtic Park would pull him and his friends away from honing their skills in Soho Street.

For his debut, he managed to catch the last ever half-hour of the last ever old-style Scottish First Division match played at Celtic Park on Saturday, April 19, 1975, before league reconstruction and the new Scottish Premier Division came into being. The downside is that Celtic lost 2-1 to a Dundee side featuring Lisbon Lion Tommy Gemmell.

For the young Celtic midfielder, it represented the very first step on what turned out to be an extraordinary career with the club, though he couldn't have known that at the time. He was just glad to have pulled on the famous green and white hooped jersey for the first time.

It was in the 1980s that he established himself as a vital player for the club, helping deliver a number of memorable triumphs for Celtic, not least the centenary double triumph. And he always understood what it meant to supporters, famously stating: 'When you pull on that jersey, you're not just playing for a football club, you're playing for a people and a cause.'

Tommy Burns won six championship medals, the first of those being Jock Stein's last success with the double of season 1976/77 and the last being the glorious centenary double of 1987/88.

Burns was also part of the squad which won the league in 1979, to give Billy McNeill his first title as Celtic manager, though he missed out on the '10-men-won-the-league' game through injury. There were successive championships in 1981 and '82, with Burns scoring the winner at Tannadice to clinch the first of those two titles. And then there were the memorable triumphs of 1986 at Love Street and two years later in the club's centenary season.

Add in four Scottish Cup triumphs and a League Cup win in 1982 and it was an impressive haul of winner's medals for the player, though such were the demands he put on himself and his team-mates, he would have been disappointed not to have gained even more.

When he left in 1989, he went on to establish a great reputation at Kilmarnock, as a player and then as manager, and Kilmarnock's continued presence in the top flight of Scottish football has its foundations in Burns' tenure as manager.

For Tommy Burns, however, Celtic was always the great football love of his life, and he would return to Paradise in 1994, laying the foundations for the future success that Celtic enjoyed, although his team would only win one solitary trophy, the Scottish Cup in 1995.

His team played football 'the Celtic way', enthralling, exciting, and even sometimes infuriating supporters, but there was pride and passion in wearing the Hoops and in knowing what they represent to so many people.

TOMMY BURNS

MIDFIELDER
Celtic debut:
April 19, 1975, League,
Celtic 1-2 Dundee
(substitute)

	App	Subs	Goals
League	324	32	52
Scottish Cup	38	5	12
League Cup	70	0	15
Europe	31	3	3
Total	**463**	**40**	**82**

> He had a rather short road to Paradise as he lived not far along the road in the Calton district of Glasgow

TOMMY BURNS

STORY OF OUR LEGENDS

JIM BROGAN
1962 - 1975

As a player, Jim Brogan is perhaps the definition of 'unsung hero'. He played 341 times for Celtic, winning a total of 14 honours with the club during a 12-year period.

He made his debut as far back as 1963, but it wasn't until the 1968/69 season that he could be considered a first-team regular. He played in a European Cup final. Unfortunately for him, it was the 1970 final in Milan, which Celtic lost to Feyenoord after extra-time. He could rightly be considered an integral part of the club's nine-in-a-row success, playing in seven of those nine championship triumphs, while there were four Scottish Cups and three League Cups to boast of.

Yet, if his name has not been completely lost, it is sometimes forgotten, dropping between the cracks of the Lisbon Lions and the Quality Street Gang, the full-backs of Craig and Gemmell, and then Danny McGrain eclipsing a player who gave first-class service to the Hoops over many years.

He followed in the footsteps of his older brother, Frank, who had joined Celtic in 1960, and the two brothers were in the same team when Jim made his debut for the club. Frank left in 1964 after making 48 appearances and scoring 17 goals for the club. Jim, meanwhile, remained at Celtic Park, and slowly but surely pushed his way into Jock Stein's first-team squad, where he would remain until the mid-1970s. He remained shy of the limelight, both as a player and after he retired from the game, though he would enjoy more success as a businessman in the years after he hung up his boots.

The younger Brogan enjoyed a very successful Celtic career, the reward for hard-work, perseverance and plenty of patience. Although he made a number of appearances in the first team, Brogan had to wait until 1968, and an injury to regular sweeper John Clark, for an extended run in the top-team. After that, though, he never looked back.

At the end of that season, Brogan collected his first of many winner's medals when Celtic secured the league championship and then the Scottish Cup, with a fantastic 4-0 victory over Rangers. From there on, it was Lisbon Lion, Clark that was used sparingly, as the tough and resolute Brogan formed a formidable partnership with Billy McNeill at the heart of the Celtic defence, which would be the base for a continued domination of Scottish football for years to come.

The defender was someone that relished the physical challenges of the game, such as the memorable European Cup semi-final triumph over Leeds United at Hampden in 1970. And in 1971, his outstanding performances were recognised when he was runner-up to Martin Buchan as the Scottish Player of the Year.

In 1975, aged 31, and with increasing competition for his place, Jim Brogan eventually left Celtic. Jock Stein handed him the captaincy for his final game, the Glasgow Cup final match against Rangers, on May 10, 1975, which finished 2-2. The game also celebrated Glasgow's 800th birthday and both teams shared the trophy. Typically, he finished the match nursing a broken rib.

His next destination would be Coventry City, spending 18 months there, before moving back north for a spell with Ayr United to finish his career.

JIM BROGAN

RIGHT-BACK
Celtic debut:
September 21, 1963,
League,
Falkirk 1-0 Celtic

	App	Subs	Goals
League	208	5	6
Scottish Cup	37	1	0
League Cup	55	2	2
Europe	32	1	1
Total	**332**	**9**	**9**

JOE McBRIDE
1965 - 1968

On four separate occasions, Celtic had been linked with a move for Joe McBride but for various reasons they just never materialised. But several clubs and many goals later, the striker joined his boyhood idols in 1965 from Motherwell following spells with Kilmarnock, Wolves, Luton Town and Partick Thistle as Jock Stein's first signing.

If McBride had to wait a long time to fulfil his Celtic dream, it was well worth it as he quickly made up for lost time by joining just as the Hoops began their domination of Scottish football and then the continent.

Still, when you recite the story of McBride, you cannot help thinking of what might have been.

Up until December 1967, the striker's goal-scoring stats were simply phenomenal. In that season alone, McBride had plundered 36 goals by Christmas. But his campaign was cut short by a serious knee injury in a match with Aberdeen.

That was the sort of striking acumen that had Joe only behind the great Jimmy McGrory in goal-scoring prowess or, to put

it in more modern terms, his goal-scoring record on a game-to-game ratio was even better than that of Henrik Larsson.

Given that he challenged McGrory for the title of Celtic's most precocious striker, it's no surprise that McGrory himself described McBride as the best goalscorer he had seen at the club – no mean compliment from the best of all and a man who had been watching Celtic score goals for the best part of half-a-century.

The December injury would rule him out of the European Cup triumph in Lisbon six months later and, eventually, end his Celtic career.

His goals in the opening rounds of the European Cup did make him a much-valued member of the Lisbon Lions' squad, though, and his truly amazing goals-per-game ratio during Celtic's greatest ever season was a key component of the team's unrivalled success in 1966/67 and he also picked up two Scottish League championship and two League Cup medals, from his Hoops career.

With a goal-scoring record as impressive as McBride, it's no surprise there is no shortage of hat-tricks to reminisce about. In total, he struck nine in two-and-a-half seasons. A remarkable total considering he spent 12 months of that out injured.

Despite making a successful comeback from injury, McBride found it hard to win back a place in the starting XI due to the tremendous form of Willie Wallace and Stevie Chalmers.

His relatively short stint at the club came in the Hoops' greatest and most silver-laden period and in his 93 games he scored an amazing 86 goals.

In November 1968, Stein sold the striker on to Hibernian, where he was top scorer for the next two seasons.

He also returned to haunt the Hoops when he played against them. So much so that the great Jock Stein had to admit to the player himself that he probably let him go a bit early.

He departed Easter Road in 1971, and after spells at Dunfermline and Clyde, McBride drew the curtain on a distinguished playing career.

JOE McBRIDE
FORWARD
Celtic debut:
August 21, 1965,
League Cup,
Celtic 0-2 Dundee United

	App	Subs	Goals
League	52	3	54
Scottish Cup	8	0	3
League Cup	21	0	24
Europe	9	0	5
Total	**90**	**3**	**86**

MADE IN PARADISE | 89

STORY OF OUR LEGENDS

BERTIE AULD

1955 - 1961, 1965 - 1971

Having joined Celtic in 1955, Bertie had a loan spell with Dumbarton before returning to the club, and prior to making his league debut, he played in a Charity Cup match against Rangers on May 1, 1957.

It would be just a few months later, however, that the Hoops would record their famous 7-1 victory over Rangers in the League Cup final.

That was one honour he missed out on, though, as he was omitted for the final despite playing against every side up until that game. He was left out in favour of Neilly Mochan. The 7-1 victory over Rangers in the final seemed to vindicate the team selection, and though disappointed to have missed out on the famous victory, Bertie has always been magnanimous to admit that the more experienced Mochan deserved his place in the team.

He was with the club until 1961 when he left to join Birmingham City and spent almost four years in England before returning to Celtic Park in January 1965, just two months before Jock Stein returned to the club as manager. Bertie Auld would be an integral part of the success Celtic enjoyed over the next few seasons.

The 1965 Scottish Cup triumph was a pivotal moment in Celtic's history as, within a few weeks of being made manager, Jock Stein was leading his team to victory in the final at Hampden against Dunfermline. It was a tough game against a side who had beaten Celtic in the final four years previously, when Stein was manager of the Pars. The Fifers were twice ahead in the match but both times Bertie Auld scored to draw Celtic level. And then, with nine minutes remaining, Billy McNeill headed home a Charlie Gallagher corner to give Celtic a 3-2 victory.

Bertie was, of course, part of the Lisbon Lions, and over and above his skill, passion and tenacity on the football field, will be forever remembered in the Celtic history books as the man who started singing *The Celtic Song* in the tunnel at Lisbon before the European Cup final in 1967, much to the bemusement of the Inter Milan players.

He and Bobby Murdoch formed a formidable partnership in the heart of the Celtic team, and there could have been few better midfield duos playing in football during the 1960s and early '70s than Murdoch and Auld.

Bertie made a total of 275 appearances for the Hoops, scoring 78 goals during his two spells at Celtic. His first competitive goal came on August 28, 1957 in a League Cup sectional game against East Fife at Celtic Park. The Hoops won that match 6-1 in front of a crowd of 18,000, with Bertie scoring on 32 minutes. His last competitive goal in Celtic colours came at Dens Park in a 2-1 victory over Dundee on April 6, 1970.

The club legend won a total of 13 major honours during his time with Celtic – five league championships, three Scottish Cups, four League Cups and, of course, the European Cup in 1967.

> Bertie will be forever remembered as the man who started singing *The Celtic Song* before the European Cup final in 1967, much to the bemusement of the Inter Milan players

BERTIE AULD

OUTSIDE-LEFT/ MIDFIELD
Celtic debut:
August 24, 1957,
League Cup,
Airdrie 1-2 Celtic

	App	Subs	Goals
League	167	9	50
Scottish Cup	26	2	8
League Cup	42	5	20
Europe	22	2	0
Total	**257**	**18**	**78**

STORY OF OUR LEGENDS

SEAN FALLON

1950 - 1958

Sean Fallon was born in Sligo on July 31, 1922. As a player, he wore the Hoops between 1950 and 1958, making 254 appearances and scoring 14 goals. He was also capped eight times by the Republic of Ireland.

Sean's footballing career started with St Mary's Juniors, Sligo, and he also played Gaelic football for Craobh Ruadh. He went on to play for McArthurs, Sligo Distillery and Longford Town before he arrived at the Showgrounds in 1947 to play for Rovers.

He then joined Glenavon in the north before impressing Celtic with his performance for the Irish League against the League of Ireland.

Sean Fallon's Celtic connection started when Joe McMenemy, son of Jimmy McMenemy, saved Fallon's sister from drowning. McMenemy was invited back to the Fallons' house, and Joe sent Sean a Celtic shirt and a copy of Willie Maley's book, *The Story of the Celtic*.

The Irishman went on to realise his ambition of playing for Celtic when he made his league debut for the Hoops, away to Clyde, in the last game of the 1949/50 season. At the end of season 1950/51, he earned his first piece of silverware by helping Celtic beat Motherwell in the Scottish Cup final.

By October 1953, Sean had been made club captain but broke a collarbone against Hearts which sidelined him for part of the season. In his absence, the captaincy was passed on to Jock Stein – at Sean's request.

At the end of season 1953/54, Celtic had secured the league and cup double, with Sean scoring in the 2-1 victory over Aberdeen at Hampden to clinch the Scottish Cup.

And he was also part

of the famous team which retained the League Cup in 1957, as Celtic beat Rangers 7-1. The club had won it for the first time in the previous season against Partick Thistle.

In 1958, injury finally got the better of Sean and forced him to call time on his playing days but it was far from the end of his association with Celtic, becoming an important member

of the coaching staff. When Robert Kelly decided to bring Jock Stein to Paradise in 1965, the initial proposal was that Stein would act as Sean Fallon's assistant. However, Stein would only return on condition that he would be No.1 with complete authority over all team matters.

The Celtic chairman eventually relented and offered Stein the job, and the first thing that the new manager did was ask Sean, who was Jock Stein's great friend in the Celtic dressing room during his playing days, to be his assistant. It was a potent partnership which transformed Celtic into the dominant force in Scotland and to European success 1967. Sean never aired any disappointment at this decision, stating once again that he was happy to serve 'my club' in any role he was asked.

Over the years, he was responsible was bringing players like Tommy Gemmell, David Hay, Danny McGrain, Kenny Dalgish, Lou Macari and Packie Bonner to Celtic.

The phrase 'Celtic legend' is one that easily applies to Sean Fallon. For 28 years, he served the club faithfully as a player and then as an integral part of the management team, playing an instrumental role in the incredible successes of the 1960s and '70s.

SEAN FALLON

FORWARD

Celtic debut:
April 15, 1950,
League,
Clyde 2-2 Celtic

	App	Subs	Goals
League	178	n/a	8
Scottish Cup	30	n/a	2
League Cup	47	n/a	3
Europe	n/a	n/a	n/a
Total	**255**	**n/a**	**13**

SHUNSUKE NAKAMURA
2005 - 2009

Like the previous Celtic No.25 before him, Shunsuke Nakamura arrived at the club as somewhat of an unknown.

Standing at 5' 10" and of slight build, many wondered how the Japanese playmaker would handle the robust nature of the Scottish game but, just like his predecessor, Lubo Moravcik, few were left doubting after Nakamura's first season at the Celts.

The Far East star was signed by Gordon Strachan in 2005 from Serie A side Reggina and was heralded by the Hoops manager as a player with incredible vision.

His passing and distribution under pressure were soon found to be unparalleled in Scotland and his dynamic approach to the game, encapsulated in his Man of the Match performance on his debut against Dundee United, rendered any aspersions about his overall ability redundant.

Nakamura went on to win the SPFL Premiership and Scottish League Cup in his first season but it was in his second season at the club that he truly shined.

After a disappointing first European campaign for Strachan's side, Nakamura radically transformed Celtic's fortunes on the continent.

His curling free-kick at Old Trafford against Manchester United in September 2006 saw him become the first Japanese player to score in the competition, but it was the incredible 30-yard set-piece effort against United two months later at Celtic Park that will be remembered most fondly by the Hoops support as it carried the Bhoys into the knockout stages of the tournament for the first time.

Nakamura's dead ball dexterity continued throughout the season and it was through another of his magical free-kicks that the Celts eventually won the league title, with his stoppage time goal proving the decider in a dramatic 2-1 win over Kilmarnock at Rugby Park.

His performances in his second season saw Nakamura named the SPFA, SFWA, Player and Players' Player of the Year while his exquisitely chipped goal against Dundee United in a tense Boxing Day draw was also named Goal of the Season.

His penultimate season at Paradise was hampered by injury in the opening months but Nakamura made a scoring return to action in the Scottish Cup before becoming the first Japanese player to find the net in a Glasgow derby with an incredible long-range strike against Celtic's city rivals.

A hat-trick against St Mirren in a 7-0 win capped off the Japanese icon's final season in style but it will always be Nakamura's outstanding passing ability, close control and, mostly, his stunning accuracy from free-kicks that Celtic fans will remember.

He left the club in the summer of 2009 to join Espanyol in La Liga before returning, as promised, to Yokohama F Marinos in his homeland, where he became captain and continued to win matches with his sensational set-pieces.

SHUNSUKE NAKAMURA

MIDFIELDER
Celtic debut:
August 6, 2005,
League,
Celtic 2-0 Dundee United

	App	Subs	Goals
League	121	7	29
Scottish Cup	7	0	1
League Cup	12	0	1
Europe	17	2	2
Total	**157**	**9**	**33**

A MAGAZINE MADE IN PARADISE

SUBSCRIBE BY DIRECT DEBIT FOR ONLY £8 PER MONTH

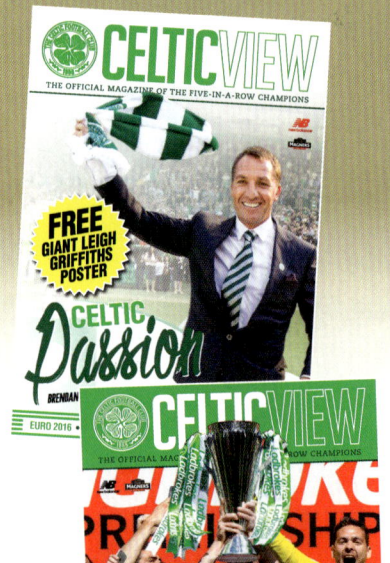

NEW MANAGER SPEAKS EXCLUSIVELY TO THE CELTIC VIEW

CELTIC VIEW SUBSCRIPTION OPTIONS

£8 PER MONTH DIRECT DEBIT (CALL 0845 301 7627)

- 10 issues (UK) £24.50
- 20 issues (UK) £47
- 45 issues (UK) £101.25

Above prices include free P&P

Every magazine delivered direct to your door
Overseas prices available online
Prices subject to change

TO SUBSCRIBE CALL 0845 301 7627
OR LOG ON TO CELTICFC.NET/PUBLICATIONS

Send a cheque payable to Sport Media to: Celtic Publications, PO Box 48, Old Hall Street, Liverpool, L69 3EB

celticpublications@sportmedia-tm.com

Trinity Mirror Sport Media

ALSO AVAILABLE DIGITALLY AT WWW.MAGZTER.COM

STORY OF OUR LEGENDS

BANNER BHOYS
STATISTICS

1888 - 2016

JIMMY JOHNSTONE
WINGER
Celtic debut: March 27, 1963, League, Kilmarnock 6-0 Celtic

	App	Subs	Goals
League	298	10	82
Scottish Cup	47	1	11
League Cup	87	5	21
Europe	66	1	16
Total	**498**	**17**	**130**

JOHNNY DOYLE
FORWARD
Celtic debut: March 20, 1976, League, Dundee 0-1 Celtic

	App	Subs	Goals
League	82	13	15
Scottish Cup	10	2	7
League Cup	25	4	14
Europe	6	1	1
Total	**123**	**20**	**37**

JOHN COLLINS
MIDFIELDER
Celtic debut: August 22, 1990 League Cup Celtic 4-0 Airdrie

	App	Subs	Goals
League	211	6	47
Scottish Cup	21	0	3
League Cup	22	0	3
Europe	13	0	1
Total	**267**	**6**	**54**

STEVIE CHALMERS
FORWARD
Celtic debut: March 10, 1959, League, Celtic 1-2 Airdrie

	App	Subs	Goals
League	253	8	158
Scottish Cup	45	2	33
League Cup	57	2	27
Europe	38	1	13
Total	**393**	**13**	**231**

NEILLY MOCHAN
OUTSIDE-LEFT
Celtic debut: August 8, 1953, League Cup, Celtic 0-1 Aberdeen

	App	Subs	Goals
League	191	n/a	81
Scottish Cup	34	n/a	16
League Cup	43	n/a	12
Europe	n/a	n/a	n/a
Total	**268**	**n/a**	**109**

DIXIE DEANS
FORWARD
Celtic debut: November 27, 1971, League, Partick Thistle 1-5 Celtic (scored once)

	App	Subs	Goals
League	122	5	89
Scottish Cup	21	0	18
League Cup	21	1	11
Europe	11	3	6
Total	**175**	**9**	**124**

KENNY DALGLISH
FORWARD
Celtic debut: September 25, 1968, League Cup, Hamilton Accies 2-4 Celtic

	App	Subs	Goals
League	200	4	112
Scottish Cup	30	0	11
League Cup	56	3	35
Europe	27	0	9
Total	**313**	**7**	**167**

JOHN HUGHES
FORWARD
Celtic debut: August 13, 1960, League Cup, Celtic 2-0 Third Lanark (scored once)

	App	Subs	Goals
League	233	3	115
Scottish Cup	42	1	25
League Cup	62	1	38
Europe	40	1	10
Total	**377**	**6**	**188**

BOBBY MURDOCH
MIDFIELDER
Celtic debut: August 11, 1962, League Cup, Celtic 3-1 Hearts (scored once)

	App	Subs	Goals
League	287	4	61
Scottish Cup	84	0	17
League Cup	53	0	13
Europe	57	0	11
Total	**481**	**4**	**102**

JOHN FALLON
GOALKEEPER
Celtic debut: September 26, 1959, League, Celtic 1-1 Clyde

	App	Subs	Goals
League	125	0	0
Scottish Cup	14	0	0
League Cup	36	0	0
Europe	20	0	0
Total	**195**	**0**	**0**

STORY OF OUR LEGENDS

JIMMY McGRORY
CENTRE-FORWARD
Celtic debut:
January 20, 1923,
League,
Third Lanark 1-0 Celtic

	App	Subs	Goals
League	378	n/a	395
Scottish Cup	67	n/a	73
League Cup	n/a	n/a	n/a
Europe	n/a	n/a	n/a
Total	445	n/a	468

JIM CRAIG
RIGHT-BACK
Celtic debut:
October 10, 1965,
European Cup-Winners'
Cup, Celtic 1-0 Go Ahead
Deventer

	App	Subs	Goals
League	143	4	1
Scottish Cup	21	2	0
League Cup	29	1	4
Europe	31	0	1
Total	224	7	6

BOBBY LENNOX
OUTSIDE-LEFT
Celtic debut:
March 3, 1962
League,
Celtic 2-1 Dundee

	App	Subs	Goals
League	297	49	170
Scottish Cup	46	5	31
League Cup	107	13	62
Europe	57	12	14
Total	507	79	277

PAT BONNER
GOALKEEPER
Celtic debut:
March 17, 1979,
League,
Celtic 2-1 Motherwell

	App	Subs	Goals
League	483	0	0
Scottish Cup	55	0	0
League Cup	64	0	0
Europe	39	0	0
Total	641	0	0

ROY AITKEN
MIDFIELDER
Celtic debut:
April 4, 1984,
League,
Rangers 1-0 Celtic

	App	Subs	Goals
League	483	0	40
Scottish Cup	55	0	2
League Cup	82	2	6
Europe	50	0	4
Total	670	2	52

CHRIS SUTTON
FORWARD
Celtic debut:
July 31, 2000,
League Cup,
Dundee United 1-2
Celtic (scored once)

	App	Subs	Goals
League	127	3	60
Scottish Cup	16	0	5
League Cup	8	1	2
Europe	41	2	16
Total	192	6	83

SANDY McMAHON
INSIDE-LEFT
Celtic debut:
January 24, 1891,
League,
Vale of Leven 3-1 Celtic

	App	Subs	Goals
League	174	n/a	130
Scottish Cup	43	n/a	47
League Cup	n/a	n/a	n/a
Europe	n/a	n/a	n/a
Total	217	n/a	177

STILIYAN PETROV
MIDFIELDER
Celtic debut:
August 13, 1999,
League,
Dundee United 2-1 Celtic

	App	Subs	Goals
League	172	13	55
League Cup	9	5	0
Scottish Cup	15	3	5
Europe	49	2	4
Total	245	23	64

JIMMY DELANEY
**OUTSIDE-RIGHT/
CENTRE-FORWARD**
Celtic debut:
August 18, 1934, League,
Hearts 0-0 Celtic

	App	Subs	Goals
League	143	n/a	69
Scottish Cup	17	n/a	5
League Cup	n/a	n/a	n/a
Europe	n/a	n/a	n/a
Total	160	n/a	74

BRIAN McCLAIR
FORWARD
Celtic debut:
August 24, 1983,
League Cup,
Brechin City 0-1 Celtic

	App	Subs	Goals
League	129	16	99
Scottish Cup	14	4	11
League Cup	19	1	9
Europe	13	3	2
Total	175	24	121

CHARLIE TULLY
INSIDE-LEFT
Celtic debut:
November 27, 1971,
League,
Partick Thistle 1-5 Celtic

	App	Subs	Goals
League	216	n/a	30
Scottish Cup	35	n/a	6
League Cup	68	n/a	7
Europe	n/a	n/a	n/a
Total	319	n/a	43

JACKIE McNAMARA
RIGHT-BACK
Celtic debut:
October 4, 1995,
League,
Falkirk 0-1 Celtic

	App	Subs	Goals
League	221	36	10
Scottish Cup	25	5	3
League Cup	17	2	1
Europe	43	9	1
Total	307	52	15

PATSY GALLACHER
INSIDE-RIGHT
Celtic debut:
December 2, 1911,
League,
Celtic 3-1 St Mirren

	App	Subs	Goals
League	432	n/a	186
Scottish Cup	32	n/a	6
League Cup	n/a	n/a	n/a
Europe	n/a	n/a	n/a
Total	464	n/a	192

DAVIE HAY
MIDFIELDER
Celtic debut:
March 6, 1968
(substitute), League,
Celtic 4-1 Aberdeen

	App	Subs	Goals
League	106	3	6
Scottish Cup	24	0	1
League Cup	37	0	5
Europe	23	0	0
Total	190	3	12

PAUL LAMBERT
MIDFIELDER
Celtic debut:
August 11, 1997,
League,
Rangers 1-0 Celtic

	App	Subs	Goals
League	180	12	14
Scottish Cup	19	4	1
League Cup	10	1	2
Europe	44	3	2
Total	253	20	19

ALEC McNAIR
UTILITY/RIGHT-BACK
Celtic debut:
January 3, 1905,
League,
Celtic 2-3 Airdrie

	App	Subs	Goals
League	584	n/a	9
Scottish Cup	57	n/a	0
League Cup	n/a	n/a	n/a
Europe	n/a	n/a	n/a
Total	641	n/a	9

PAUL McSTAY

MIDFIELDER
Celtic debut:
January 23, 1982,
Scottish Cup,
Celtic 4-0
Queen of the South

	App	Subs	Goals
League	509	6	57
Scottish Cup	66	0	6
League Cup	54	0	7
Europe	42	0	2
Total	**671**	**6**	**72**

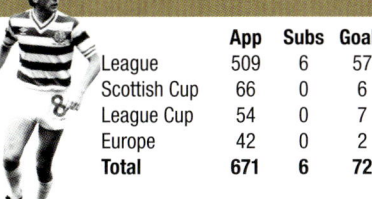

NEIL LENNON

MIDFIELDER
Celtic debut:
December 10, 2000,
League,
Dundee 1-2 Celtic

	App	Subs	Goals
League	212	2	3
Scottish Cup	26	0	0
League Cup	10	1	0
Europe	52	1	0
Total	**300**	**4**	**3**

WILLIE FERNIE

INSIDE-FORWARD
Celtic debut:
March 18, 1950,
League,
St Mirren 0-1 Celtic

	App	Subs	Goals
League	219	n/a	54
Scottish Cup	39	n/a	10
League Cup	59	n/a	11
Europe	n/a	n/a	n/a
Total	**317**	**n/a**	**75**

RONNIE SIMPSON

GOALKEEPER
Celtic debut:
November 18, 1964,
Fairs Cities' Cup,
Barcelona 3-1 Celtic

	App	Subs	Goals
League	118	0	0
Scottish Cup	17	0	0
League Cup	29	0	0
Europe	24	0	0
Total	**188**	**0**	**0**

DANNY McGRAIN

RIGHT-BACK
Celtic debut:
August 26, 1970
(substitute),
League Cup,
Dundee United 2-2 Celtic

	App	Subs	Goals
League	433	8	4
Scottish Cup	60	0	1
League Cup	105	1	3
Europe	55	1	0
Total	**653**	**10**	**8**

WILLIE WALLACE

STRIKER
Celtic debut:
December 10, 1966,
League,
Celtic 4-2 Motherwell

	App	Subs	Goals
League	135	6	88
Scottish Cup	24	2	21
League Cup	31	5	12
Europe	27	2	13
Total	**217**	**15**	**134**

PETER GRANT

MIDFIELDER
Celtic debut:
April 4, 1984, League,
Rangers 1-0 Celtic

	App	Subs	Goals
League	338	26	15
Scottish Cup	34	4	1
League Cup	40	3	3
Europe	32	1	0
Total	**444**	**34**	**19**

WILLIE O'NEILL

FULL-BACK
Celtic debut:
April 26, 1961,
Scottish Cup,
Dunfermline 2-0 Celtic

	App	Subs	Goals
League	49	1	0
Scottish Cup	3	0	0
League Cup	18	2	0
Europe	9	0	0
Total	**79**	**3**	**0**

MURDO MacLEOD

MIDFIELDER
Celtic debut:
November 4, 1978,
League,
Celtic 1-2 Motherwell

	App	Subs	Goals
League	274	7	55
Scottish Cup	36	2	7
League Cup	44	0	13
Europe	32	0	7
Total	**386**	**9**	**82**

LUBO MORAVCIK

MIDFIELDER
Celtic debut:
November 7, 1998,
League,
Celtic 6-1 Dundee

	App	Subs	Goals
League	75	19	29
Scottish Cup	9	1	1
League Cup	8	2	2
Europe	11	4	3
Total	**103**	**26**	**35**

JOHN CLARK

LEFT-HALF
Celtic debut:
October 3, 1959,
Scottish League,
Arbroath 0-5 Celtic

	App	Subs	Goals
League	185	1	1
Scottish Cup	30	1	1
League Cup	60	2	1
Europe	37	0	0
Total	**312**	**4**	**3**

BERTIE PEACOCK

LEFT-HALF
Celtic debut:
September 29, 1949,
League Cup,
Celtic 1-3 Aberdeen

	App	Subs	Goals
League	319	n/a	32
Scottish Cup	56	n/a	8
League Cup	80	n/a	10
Europe	n/a	n/a	n/a
Total	**455**	**n/a**	**50**

TOM BOYD

DEFENDER
Celtic debut:
February 8, 1992,
League,
Celtic 2-0 Airdrie

	App	Subs	Goals
League	296	10	2
Scottish Cup	31	3	0
League Cup	31	2	0
Europe	33	1	0
Total	**391**	**16**	**2**

BOBBY EVANS

RIGHT-HALF, CENTRE-HALF
Celtic debut: August 19, 1944, Regional League, Albion Rovers 0-1 Celtic

	App	Subs	Goals
League	385	n/a	10
Scottish Cup	64	n/a	0
League Cup	88	n/a	1
Europe	n/a	n/a	n/a
Total	**537**	**n/a**	**11**

JIMMY McMENEMY

INSIDE-LEFT
Celtic debut:
September 29, 1902,
League,
Celtic 2-2 Hearts

	App	Subs	Goals
League	457	n/a	141
Scottish Cup	59	n/a	23
League Cup	n/a	n/a	n/a
Europe	n/a	n/a	n/a
Total	**516**	**n/a**	**164**

JOHN HARTSON

STRIKER
Celtic debut:
August 4, 2001, League,
Kilmarnock 0-1 Celtic

	App	Subs	Goals
League	125	21	89
Scottish Cup	11	1	8
League Cup	10	1	7
Europe	25	7	6
Total	**171**	**30**	**110**

MADE IN PARADISE

STORY OF OUR LEGENDS

BILLY McNEILL

CENTRE-HALF
Celtic debut: August 23, 1959, League Cup, Celtic 2-0 Clyde

	App	Subs	Goals
League	486	0	21
Scottish Cup	94	0	7
League Cup	138	0	4
Europe	72	0	3
Total	**790**	**0**	**35**

JOCK STEIN

CENTRE-HALF
Celtic debut: August 12, 1951, League, Celtic 2-1 St Mirren

	App	Subs	Goals
League	106	n/a	2
Scottish Cup	21	n/a	0
League Cup	21	n/a	0
Europe	n/a	n/a	n/a
Total	**148**	**n/a**	**2**

JOHN THOMSON

GOALKEEPER
Celtic debut: February 12, 1927, League, Dundee 1-2 Celtic

	App	Subs	Goals
League	163	n/a	0
Scottish Cup	25	n/a	0
League Cup	n/a	n/a	n/a
Europe	n/a	n/a	n/a
Total	**188**	**n/a**	**0**

TOMMY GEMMELL

FULL-BACK
Celtic debut: January 5, 1963, League, Aberdeen 1-5 Celtic

	App	Subs	Goals
League	247	0	38
Scottish Cup	43	0	3
League Cup	74	0	10
Europe	54	0	12
Total	**418**	**0**	**63**

WILLIE MALEY

HALF-BACK
Celtic debut: May 28, 1888, Inaugural Match, Celtic 5-2 Rangers

	App	Subs	Goals
League	75	n/a	2
Scottish Cup	25	n/a	2
League Cup	n/a	n/a	n/a
Europe	n/a	n/a	n/a
Total	**96**	**n/a**	**4**

JIMMY QUINN

CENTRE-FORWARD
Celtic debut: January 19, 1901, League, St Mirren 3-4 Celtic (scored once)

	App	Subs	Goals
League	273	n/a	187
Scottish Cup	58	n/a	30
League Cup	n/a	n/a	n/a
Europe	n/a	n/a	n/a
Total	**331**	**n/a**	**217**

CHARLIE GALLAGHER

INSIDE-FORWARD
Celtic debut: August 22, 1959, League Cup, Celtic 1-0 Raith Rovers

	App	Subs	Goals
League	107	0	17
Scottish Cup	23	0	4
League Cup	28	0	11
Europe	13	0	0
Total	**171**	**0**	**32**

HENRIK LARSSON

FORWARD
Celtic debut: August 3, 1997, League, Hibernian 2-1 Celtic

	App	Subs	Goals
League	218	3	174
Scottish Cup	25	0	23
League Cup	11	0	10
Europe	58	0	35
Total	**312**	**3**	**242**

JOHNNY CRUM

FORWARD
Celtic debut: October 22, 1932, League, Celtic 4-1 Motherwell (scored twice)

	App	Subs	Goals
League	190	n/a	73
Scottish Cup	21	n/a	14
League Cup	n/a	n/a	n/a
Europe	n/a	n/a	n/a
Total	**211**	**n/a**	**87**

SCOTT BROWN

(Stats correct up to end of season 2015/16)
MIDFIELDER
Celtic debut: August 5, 2007, League, Celtic 0-0 Kilmarnock

	App	Subs	Goals
League	236	14	24
Scottish Cup	17	2	2
League Cup	29	2	7
Europe	62	2	1
Total	**344**	**20**	**34**

TOMMY BURNS

MIDFIELDER
Celtic debut: April 19, 1975, League, Celtic 1-2 Dundee (substitute)

	App	Subs	Goals
League	324	32	52
Scottish Cup	38	5	12
League Cup	70	0	15
Europe	31	3	3
Total	**463**	**40**	**82**

JIM BROGAN

RIGHT-BACK
Celtic debut: September 21, 1963, League, Falkirk 1-0 Celtic

	App	Subs	Goals
League	208	5	6
Scottish Cup	37	1	0
League Cup	55	2	2
Europe	32	1	1
Total	**332**	**9**	**9**

JOE McBRIDE

FORWARD
Celtic debut: August 21, 1965, League Cup, Celtic 0-2 Dundee United

	App	Subs	Goals
League	52	3	54
Scottish Cup	8	0	3
League Cup	21	0	24
Europe	9	0	5
Total	**90**	**3**	**86**

BERTIE AULD

OUTSIDE-LEFT/ MIDFIELD
Celtic debut: August 24, 1957, League Cup, Airdrie 1-2 Celtic

	App	Subs	Goals
League	167	9	50
Scottish Cup	26	2	8
League Cup	42	5	20
Europe	22	2	0
Total	**257**	**18**	**78**

SEAN FALLON

FORWARD
Celtic debut: April 15, 1950, League, Clyde 2-2 Celtic

	App	Subs	Goals
League	178	n/a	8
Scottish Cup	30	n/a	2
League Cup	47	n/a	3
Europe	n/a	n/a	n/a
Total	**255**	**n/a**	**13**

SHUNSUKE NAKAMURA
MIDFIELDER
Celtic debut: August 6, 2005, League, Celtic 2-0 Dundee United

	App	Subs	Goals
League	121	7	29
Scottish Cup	7	0	1
League Cup	12	0	1
Europe	17	2	2
Total	**157**	**9**	**33**